MW01124413

The Greatest Reviews I've Ever Read

BY CAROL HOENIG

Published by Three Ws

ISBN: 978-0-578-99023-1

eBook: 978-0-578-99024-8

Contents

Movies Mentioned or Reviewed

I. What Makes a Critic?

Lilies of the Field
The Wizard of Oz
All the King's Men
Goodbye, Mr. Chips
Network
The Graduate
Rocky
Somebody Up There Likes Me
The African Queen
The Night of The Hunter
Funny Girl
Annie
The Way We Were
Steel Magnolias
Shampoo
The Sun Sets in Hell
Who's Afraid of Virginia Woolf
In the Heat of the Night
The Execution of Private Slovik
Kiss of Death
Bound for Glory
Midnight Express

II. Raising the Hackles

The Sunshine Boys
Come Blow Your Horn
The Odd Couple
Soylent Green
The Omega Man
White Lightning
The End
Shamus
The Longest Yard
Smokey and the Bandit
The End
Gator
Semi-Tough
Riverboat
Love Story
Hooper
The Birds
Psycho
North by Northwest
Dial M for Murder
Rear Window
Frenzy
The Getaway
The Godfather
The Westerner (TV series)
The Nutty Professor
Cinderfella
A Few Good Men
The Great Gatsby
Catch-22
Lost Horizon
Jonathan Livingston Seagull

Death Race 2000
Who'll Stop the Rain
Five Fingers of Death
Aliens
Raging Bull
Star Wars
Alice's Adventures in Wonderland
The Wizard of Oz
Bambi
Deep Throat
Grace and Frankie (Netflix series)
The Newsroom (HBO series)
On Golden Pond
Comes a Horseman
The Parallax View
Barry Lyndon

III. John of All Trades

The Sugarland Express
Jaws
Earthquake
Towering Inferno
Exorcist
Close Encounters of the Third Kind
Star Wars
Raiders of the Lost Ark
E.T. the Extra-Terrestrial
Schindler's List
The Shop on Main Street
My Girl
The Deer Hunter
The Godfather
Godfather Part II
Last Tango in Paris
He Who Must Die
The Killing
Malizia
A Man and a Woman
Paths of Glory
Johnny Get Your Gun
Z
The Battle of Algiers
The Shining
2001: A Space Odyssey
Spartacus
Dr. Strangelove
Citizen Kane
Barry Lyndon
Great Gatsby
Taxi Driver
Enter the Dragon
Alice Doesn't Live Here Anymore
The Wizard of Oz
Black Sunday
Once Upon a Time in Hollywood
Pulp Fiction
Play It Again, Sam
The Front
Annie Hall
Match Point
Psycho
Allen V. Farrow (HBO documentary)
Soylent Green

IV. Comparing Notes

Network

Deep Throat

Great Gatsby

Philadelphia Story

Hereafter

Gran Torino

The Jazz Singer

JFK

The American Media and the 2nd Assassination of John F. Kennedy

American Graffiti

The Andy Griffith Show (TV series)

The Courtship of Eddie's Father

Happy Days (TV series)

THX 1138

Lady Sings the Blues

Imitation of Life

The United States vs. Billie Holiday (Hulu)

A Star is Born

Lady Sings the Blues

The Hiding Place

Jesus Christ Superstar

Fiddler on the Roof

Godspell

Close Encounters of the Third Kind

Star Wars

Wizard of Oz

All the President's Men

Lipstick

Death Wish

Manhattan

Deep Throat

The Sound of Music

A Chorus Line (Broadway)

Saturday Night Fever

The Boy in the Plastic Bubble

Flashdance

Footloose

Welcome Back, Kotter (TV series)

Beach Blanket Bingo

Grease

The Goodbye Girl

Richard III

The Parallax View

Saturday Night Live (TV show)

King Kong

Mighty Joe Young

Godzilla vs. Kong

Deep Throat

V. Movies I Didn't See…And Wish I Had

The Sting

Save the Tiger

Pocket Money

Judge Roy Bean

Serpico

One Flew Over The Cuckoo's Nest

Ratched

Grace and Frankie (Netflix series)

Dog Day Afternoon

The Godfather

Naked City (TV Series)

The Day of the Locust

Midnight Cowboy
Rocky
The Twilight Zone (TV series)
I Never Promised You a Rose Garden
Same Time, Next Year
A Place in the Sun
Next Stop, Greenwich Village
The Godfather
Silent Movie
Blazing Saddles
Mr. Hulot's Holiday
Looking for Mr. Goodbar
Dr. Kildare (TV series)
Seinfeld (TV series)
The Three Musketeers
Kansas City Bomber

VI. Movies I Didn't See…and Glad I Hadn't

Pretty Baby
Sextette
The Exorcist
Alice Doesn't Live Here Anymore
The Professional
Exorcist II: The Heretic
One Flew Over the Cuckoo's Nest
Deliverance
Portnoy's Complaint
Cancel My Reservation

VII. John Reviews Other Reviewers' Reviews

(Say that three times fast!)

Invasion of the Body Snatchers

Superman

Myra Breckenridge

Magic

Movie Movie

Days of Heaven

Comes a Horseman

Hooper

The Wiz

The Deer Hunter

Moment by Moment

VIII. Currently Showing

Avanti

Bluebeard

Cabaret

The Candidate

Child's Play

A Clockwork Orange

Coonskin

Cries and Whispers

The Culpepper Cattle Co.

Day of the Jackal

Duck, You Sucker

The Garden of the Finzi-Continis

Hard Times

Hitler: The Last Ten Days

Junior Bonner

Kansas City Bomber

Last of the Red-Hot Lovers

Let's Do It Again

The Master Gunfighter

Money, Money, Money

Money Talks

Murmur of the Heart

The Neptune Factor

The New Centurions

Adam 12 (TV series)

The Other

To Kill a Mockingbird

Paper Moon

Pat Garrett and Billy the Kid

Pete 'n' Tillie

Play It As It Lays

Portnoy's Complaint

The Possession of Joel Delaney

Prime Cut

The Public Eye

Roma

Rooster Cogburn

Scarecrow

A Separate Peace

Skyjacked

Airport

Slaughterhouse Five

Sounder

State of Siege

The Battle of Algiers
Ten from Your Show of Shows
Three Days of the Condor
The War Between Men and Women
My World and Welcome To It (TV series)
A Warm December
What's Up, Doc
The Valachi Papers
Life with Luigi (Radio sitcom)
Young Winston

IX. Reviewing the Academy Awards

Paper Moon
Bridge on the River Kwai
Charlie's Angels (TV series)
Planet of the Apes
Annie Hall
Looking for Mr. Goodbar
The Godfather
Goodbye, Mr. Chips
Julius Caesar (Play)
Doc Martin (TV series)
Victoria (TV series)
Atlantic Crossing (TV series)
Thelma and Louise
Real People (TV show)
The JFK Assassination: The Jim Garrison Tapes (Documentary)
The American Media & The 2nd Assassination Of President John F. Kennedy (Documentary)

X. Film Critic At Large

Roots
The Boys from Brazil

Introduction

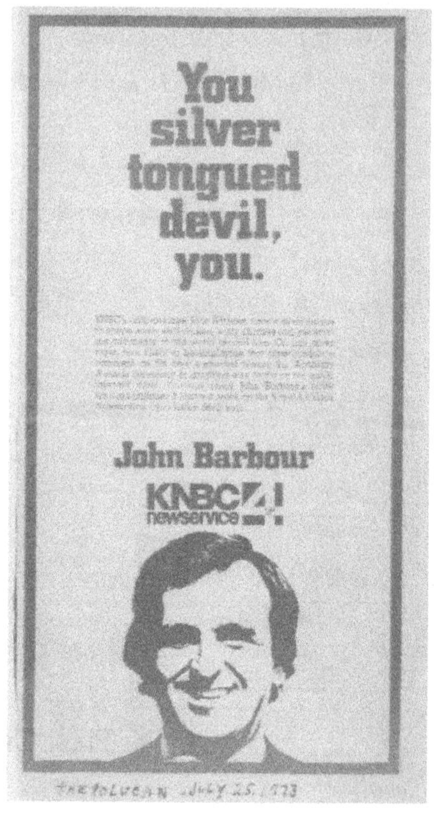

Call it kismet, serendipity or just dumb luck, but years ago when a mutual friend in the publishing industry recommended John Barbour contact me for help with his numerous endeavors, including promoting his documentary *The American Media & the 2nd Assassination of President John F. Kennedy,* editing his memoir *Your Mother's Not a Virgin: The Bumpy Life and Times of the Canadian Dropout Who Changed the Face of American TV*, and his latest book, *The Wittiest Man in America (…is a Canadian)*, I had no idea of the friendship and mutual respect that would follow. I appreciate the many traits that John has, including perseverance and passion for so many topics. I also appreciate how he never sold out, which is quite apparent in that aforementioned memoir. (While editing it, I'd find myself laughing out loud or sometimes even gasping at some of what he'd said and did without apology.)

But then something occurred to me over time while I would often check Turner Classic Movies to see what was being aired. Sometimes a movie would come on, one that I remembered John had reviewed for *LA Magazine* or when he was Critic-at-Large for five years, at KTTV for less than a year. John also reviewed more recent movies for his YouTube channel, https://johnbarboursworld.com/, but I started to think viewers would appreciate

John's thoughts and honesty regarding these movies, whether they are decades-old or newer releases. See, John isn't beholden to any network or its advertisers so he can hate or love anything he pleases and tell you why. I dare say he's one of the wittiest critics whose reviews sometimes got him in hot water; however, having had an abusive mother and absentee father, being a high school dropout, and deported back to Canada at 17 years-old, angering studio heads didn't concern John, which you'll soon discover.

But what happened to all those reviews? I asked John as much and he went into the trunk in his garage to see if he could find any. Well, folks, it was pay dirt on the day he opened that trunk. He had forgotten about all those issues with his byline where he informed readers about classics such as *Network, Grease, The Sting* and so many others.

As it happened, the timing couldn't have been better since we began working on this book during the pandemic when movie studios were in limbo and movie theaters empty. That left viewers resorting to watching old movies while waiting for new ones. That said, it is my hope when you happen upon one of the classic movies that John and I will be discussing in these pages, you'll be brought back to a time when they weren't classic but seeking positive reviews and, in turn, viewers. John was one of the few critics that could be trusted with his opinion as you will see once you begin reading.

One final note of explanation is that I have used footnotes to provide information regarding actors, directors, and producers mentioned throughout. Footnotes weren't part of John's reviews, but I felt for the younger readers or anyone hungry to know more about the film industry, they might be helpful.

Now, on with the show!

John Barbour with one of his Emmys from his reviews at KNBC

I. What Makes a Critic?

The first movie I recall going to was *Lilies of the Field* starring Sidney Poitier[1]. I had to be about eight years old. It was at a drive-in theater about twenty miles from my home. I grew up in rural Upstate New York so going anywhere was a big deal. Apparently, my mother wanted to see this movie and she never asked for much so when my father came home from work one night and had us, us being my three siblings, mother and me, climb into the car, along with a big bowl of popcorn and a thermos of Kool-Aid, it was all rather exciting.

Later, after the credits were rolling, the drive home had us all singing *Amen*, just as Poitier and the nuns had sung in the movie. What I wonder, though, was how did my mother know about this movie and what made her want to see it? The only newspaper we got was a weekly local paper and we had just three TV stations, but somehow my mom heard about the movie. Now, whenever *Lilies of the Field* airs on Turner Classic Movies, I am reminded of that night so long ago. That's what movies do: they help stir memories, whether good or bad. Mine of being cramped in the car with my family while staring at the larger-than-life movie screen in the outdoors stirs a good memory.

Another wonderful memory I have is like so many others, the one movie I looked forward to each year was *The Wizard of Oz*. Unlike now, when one can watch it several times a year or more, depending on whether they own the DVD, it was a yearly event that I would prepare myself for by claiming the best seat on the living room couch a good hour prior to the movie airing. God forbid I'd need to get up to use the bathroom or get a drink of water since my younger brother was at the ready to steal that coveted spot. No one told us about how Russell Maloney's[2] review in the August 19, 1939 issue of *The New Yorker* butchered this movie, but I don't think it would have mattered. Yes, for the very young, there were frightening scenes and John Barbour tells me that he was so scared by those angry trees throwing apples at Dorothy, Scarecrow and Tin Man that he ducked under his seat. However, that experience certainly didn't stop him from watching movies.

Unlike my limited experience in going to the theater as a child, John, who was living in Toronto, told me that movies were a major part of his childhood.

"They absolutely were," he said. "In the '30s and '40s they were a major part of everyone's life because movies were the most powerful and popular form of entertainment."

I asked, "As a child did you often go as a family?"

"I had no family," John replied. "I went by myself. I lived on the streets, on a skating rink, in police stations, libraries, but mostly in theaters. To this day I can remember scores of names of bit players. I loved movies."

I wondered what ones had the most impact on him.

"There was Broderick Crawford[3] in *All the King's Men*. Even at 12 years-old, I was impressed that movies could tell a meaningful political story. Also, Robert Donat[4] in *Goodbye, Mr. Chips*. I bawled like a baby. I still watch it today and get teary."

"Did you read as much as you saw films, John? And did you have a preference?"

"Because books were more available to me than movies, I read more. And I read everyone. O. Henry[5], Twain[6], Maugham[7], de Maupassant[8], Upton Sinclair[9]. But I preferred movies. They are the laziest art form. With a book, you have to turn a page. In a theater, you just sit there and are sucked up into the screen and become wrapped up in larger-than-life characters."

Point taken: the movies were an escape for that young boy. Therefore, I thought it made sense then that John eventually became a movie critic and asked him when was it that he decided to become one, if one can just decide to be one. His answer surprised me.

"I never decided or wanted to become one. My only dream as a kid was to become an American."

John details this desire in his delightful memoir, *Your Mother's Not a Virgin! The Bumpy Life and Times of the Canadian Dropout Who Changed the Face of American TV*. But he went on to explain:

"Like everything great in my life, it all happened by accident. Funny enough, my hero wasn't a movie star or director. My heroes were Jack Paar[10], the greatest late-night TV host ever, and Ed Murrow[11], our one and only great TV journalist. But Jack made me laugh with his perfect entertaining, intelligent talk show. I wanted to be him, so I became a standup comic. (Research shows that Jack Paar appeared as a comic in the early 1950s on The Ed Sullivan Show.) As such, I studied all the comics."

"Who were your favorites?"

"Lenny Bruce[12] and Jonathon Winters[13]. Both did great movie spoofs, especially Lenny's *Count Dracula*."

Jonathan Winters was also one of my favorites but I wasn't aware of John's success as a comic until I worked with him on his memoir. As it happens, he made two albums, *It's Tough to Be White* and *I Met A Man I Didn't Like*. I asked him how that led to him becoming a paid critic on TV for years and then at *LA Magazine*.

"In 1970, when KABC TV had their license challenged, they canceled their morning cartoons. As a suck up to the FCC they started a live news information show. Mario Machado,[14] a television and radio broadcaster and actor who all thought would get the show, suggested that I audition for a young producer named Brad Lachman.[15] On a lark, I did and got the gig. I suggested taking live phone calls from our viewers, which we did. And, here is where being a critic comes in, I suggested doing film reviews and did so three times a week.

"At the time, the GM, John McMahon, told me he didn't want me to do movie reviews because viewers only cared about what was on TV. I told him I had strong antiwar views and pro-civil rights views that I couldn't express because of The Fairness Doctrine[16] but I wanted people to know there was somebody with half a brain. So every Monday, Wednesday and Friday I did a movie review."

Anyone who has known John, knows that he does not suffer fools gladly and has strong opinions and doesn't cower under authority. Since it was the GM of the station who didn't want him doing movie reviews, I asked how he got away with doing them.

"Well, McMahon hated me, but Brad, the FCC commissioner, who guested on the show, and most importantly, the audience, loved me. It turns out that the reviews were so popular, Bob Irvine, the news director, wanted them rerun on his 6 p.m. news program. Truth is, I wasn't getting paid for these reviews and McMahon would have probably paid me not to do them because, against his will, he had to constantly defend me to the studios who threatened to cancel their movie advertising."

It caught my attention when John mentioned that he wasn't getting paid to do the reviews so when I asked him about it he said that he started getting paid after he got fired from the news program. He went on to explain:

"I booked Jim Garrison[17] to talk about his book *A Heritage of Stone* and his investigation into John F. Kennedy's assassination."

John's memoir goes into detail about this event but the short version is that John didn't have the opportunity to interview Jim Garrison, who was being sabotaged by the powers that be, because he was fired.

"But Bob Irvine still wanted the reviews on his news. I suggested to McMahon to please the viewers that I would still do them, but he responded, "Fuck the public. They don't hire you. I do."

Fortunately, Geoff Miller[18], a founder and Editor-in-Chief of *LA Magazine* called and asked John if he would consider replacing Burt Prelutsky[19] as their new film critic. Prelutsky was moving to the *LA Times*. At the time, John was still hoping to get offered a job as a TV host since he could see himself as being the next Jack Paar. However, he decided to take Miller's offer and was there for ten years where he made only $150.00 a month for a column he wrote.

"Not one raise in five years," John said. "I was barely getting $24,000.00 and yet research showed that I was responsible for ten percent of the audience. Also, I never signed a contract that they offered for five years because they would have owned my material. I did not want anyone owning it. It was not much, but it was mine."

I knew John earned a Golden Mike Award and first asked him to provide some background on what led to it. He explained, "Before I got the AM Show, Chuck Young, the GM at Metromedia's channel 11, KTTV, had given me a Saturday Night ninety-minute poor man's *Tonight Show*. I had just lost replacing Merv Griffin[20] at Westinghouse to David Frost.[21] Chuck thought Frost would bomb immediately and wanted me as a standby. Chuck was also the GM who created angry loud talkback TV by giving Joe Pyne[22] the first such TV show. By the way, on this show, I gave Redd Foxx[23] his first entertainment show appearances. Anyway, since I was now in print, I called Chuck to see if I could do the reviews on his news. I got to. I already had an Emmy for the *AM Show*, but here I won my one and only Golden Mike for Outstanding Commentary."

"So, wait," I said, "the Golden Mike wasn't for a film review then?"

"No," John replied. "It was a commentary about the 1972 massacre of Israel athletes at the Munich Olympics[24]. I was so upset after watching Johnny Carson[25] on The Tonight Show immediately afterwards and saying nothing, except for his bad jokes about Doc Severson's jacket and Ed McMahon's boozing that I wrote a piece about what it must be like to be Jewish in today's world. For two years, I raised thirty-five million for the UJA-Federation. Neil Simon[26] called to ask me to host his event at The Hilton and Tom Brokaw[27] recommended me to the news director at KNBC, and I was hired."

But what I wanted to know was, what makes one a critic? Or, more pointedly, what made John Barbour, who never graduated from high school, let alone college, with no training or formal education, a critic?

"We are all critics," John replied. "Critics of what we like and don't like. Carol, every major fucking war, excuse me for saying 'war' in front of you, but every major fucking war and financial disaster or corporate fraud in America is caused by someone with a fucking college degree or PhD."

So, what was his process in how he reviewed a movie, I wanted to know. Was it with his mind, his heart, what?

"With my ass," he said. If my ass doesn't move from the seat, it's a good film. But I try to use my mind to interpret what my ass is telling me. When I accidentally first became a critic, the two things I looked for in films were excellence in storytelling and a sense of reality. When I found them, I applauded lustily; when I did not, I attacked just as lustily. But applauding made me happier. I preferred that feeling!"

I pushed John further, asking if there were times that he was on the fence about a particular movie, which would make it more difficult to review. In other words, wouldn't a lukewarm review leave the movie-goer uncertain and cause them to lose trust in the reviewer?

"For me," John said, "I never had mixed feelings about a film. I either liked it or I did not. But if I did not like it in its entirety, I could like individual scenes, performances, or dialogue. I looked for and hoped for and expected certain things every time I sat down to watch a film. First, not to be bored, but to be engaged. Second, to learn something new. And third, originality."

As I write this book, we are nearing the end, or hopefully the end, of the Covid pandemic, which affected almost everything normal in our lives, including movie making. Movie studios shut down, theaters had to close and actors were out of work. On the other side of things, unlike when John was doing reviews, now there are numerous streaming services, including Netflix, Hulu, AppleTV, HBO Max, as well as others that offer new movies and a variety of programming. On the one hand, this is wonderful, but there are so many older movies that air on Turner Classic, as well as other stations, that I am concerned they will get lost among the new releases. Perhaps, though, some of those older movies will garner a new audience, thanks to John's analyses. For instance, even though it came out in 1976, *Network* is still a must-see film. John titled his review, *Catharsis for the 'Mad-as-Hell TV Viewer* and in the review writes, *But if ever a movie belonged to its author, it's* Network. *Paddy Chayefsky*[28] *has written the kind of staggeringly brilliant speeches that audiences love to sink their ears into.* He then concludes, *and not only should the Oscar for best screenplay be given to Chayefsky, it should be retired and brought back later as the Paddy.*

Well, *Network* did go on to win some major accolades, including four Academy Awards, in the categories of Best Actor, Peter Finch[29], Best Actress, Faye Dunaway[30], Best Supporting Actress, Beatrice Straight[31] and as John hoped, Best Original Screenplay for Paddy Chayefsky.

"So," I said to John, "certainly movies are important for a number of reasons."

"Some," he replied. Like some people. One time on the air I said that movies are like people, ninety-nine percent of them are crap, but that one magnificent one makes tolerating the others worth it!"

In talking with John, it's clear that he has high respect for writers—thankfully! I'd asked him, "Who do you think is more important to the success of a film, the writer or director?" I suppose I could have included the actor in that query, as well, but it hadn't occurred to me. "Not even close," he said. "The writer. Without a script there's nothing to direct. Name me one original director of one of Shakespeare's plays. There are just a few directors who can improve an already good script, like Mike Nichols[32] did in *The Graduate*, starting with the brilliant casting of Dustin Hoffman[33] and Ann Bancroft[34]. But directors are an old over-rated asset whose names are still mistakenly shown at the end. And you know why?"

There was no need for me to ask since John was ready to tell me.

"It was fought for billing by The Directors Guild since the days of silent movies where there were no writers, just directors. And there was no Writers Guild. If you notice on TCM (Turner Classic Movies) when they list an upcoming film, they only list the director and cast; never the writer unless it's Shakespeare or Chayefsky."

The same year that *Network* was released so was *Rocky*, the first movie of what was to be watching Sylvester Stallone in the boxing arena again and again in flick after flick. As I started reading John's review of this movie, I thought maybe he was going to crucify it, which would have upset me. The reason being, I suppose, is the memory of my son who loved that movie. Even though he was born the year it came out, once he got older and home videos were the rage, he was riveted and bopped to *Eye of the Tiger*. Therefore by the second paragraph of John's review I was relieved to read, *It's an upbeat movie—and that gives you an indication of how conditioned we have become to downbeat movies. In fact, we are so desperate for heroes that we'll make one out of a fighter who would rather just go the distance than be a winner.* Rocky *would still be an upbeat film—a remarkably well-crafted and tightly constructed one that comes out on top.*

The reason I share this review is that it brings back the topic of the writer. John writes, *Sylvester Stallone, who also plays the title role, has written a deceptively simple and smart screenplay for himself; a veritable* Somebody Up There Likes Me.

What I find interesting is that John refers to other people as writers but doesn't seem to grasp that he is a wonderful one himself. But don't listen to me. Lucille Ball has been quoted as saying, "Aside from the writers of our show, (*Here's Lucy*) my favorite writer is John Barbour. Every first of the month, Gary (Morton), my husband and I fight over who gets to read his reviews first."

But there were others in John's past who saw his potential as a writer. However, he told me that he felt writing a movie would be a conflict of interest. I reminded him of James Agee who was a film critic for *Time* and *The Nation* who went on to write the screenplay for *The African Queen* and *The Night of The Hunter.* Agee apparently didn't see a conflict of interest in being a film critic and screenwriter.

John laughed and said, "And you know who said the same thing to me? Ray Stark[35], the producer."

I wanted to know how that happened. I didn't doubt John, but found the idea of having a conversation with the producer of some of the movies I absolutely loved, including *Funny Girl, Annie, The Way We Were, Steel Magnolias*, as well as others, mind-blowing.

"Stark called one day," John said, "and asked me to join him for a private lunch in his private dining room at Warner Brothers. What a dining room. What a lunch. And what a great conversation. Ray told me he loved writers. And my reviews. He started out as a writer's agent and one of his clients was Ben Hecht[36], one of my idols because of his autobiography, *A Child of the Century*. He didn't mince words and said that nearly everything Hollywood makes is shit. Even though I didn't say it, I had to agree. But as the biggest in the business, he got the choice of the best shit. He then asked me if I were to write an original movie script, what would it be about? I don't think I hesitated and simply said, 'People,' and went on to explain that Americans seem to make movies about events. Europe makes them about people. I prefer people."

I wanted to know what the successful producer's response was.

"Well," John continued, "he asked me what kind of people. I said lovers. Let's say the couple meet at a New Year's party, then follow them until the next New Year, showing their lives, jobs and in some of those scenes show what was on TV at the time. You know, Nixon. The news. Game shows, soap operas. They would come across as real people with real lives in a real country."

Interesting, I thought, thinking that was probably when the lunch concluded, but John surprised me.

"He loved it and offered me fifty thousand to write it. Ten thousand to start, fifteen to finish and twenty-five when production began, but I turned him down."

I gasped, thinking of so many authors who would have grabbed at that opportunity and said as much. Fifty thousand isn't anything to sneeze at, especially then.

"Well, I was honest with him and said my love was TV. Live TV, explaining that it is personal and immediate. That's why I loved being a comic. You write a joke and got an immediate response. I told him my dream was to do a live TV show about real people. He wished me well. Turns out the a few years later, a film that came close to showing scenes with a lot of TV in the background was *Shampoo* with Warren Beatty[37]."

I reminded John that he did make that dream happen when he created and appeared in the 1970s TV hit *Real People*.

"And you know what?" he said. "When that happened Stark sent me a note saying, 'I'll be damned. In this dream factory, a dream actually came true!'"

I thought about all this, wondering if this young man who loved movies felt intimidated by such meetings.

"Carol, odd, but it seems the greater or more influential a Hollywood biggie was, the more comfortable I was with them. I felt at home. Where I belonged. I was aware of their talents and position, but never ever in awe. I think that's why Stark and Frank Sinatra[38] liked me, and even the biggies I occasionally bashed like Bob Hope[39], Neil Simon and Burt Reynolds[40]. But as for Ray Stark, he loved my writing; therefore, me. He knew that my second favorite American writer, next to Twain, was Ben Hecht. He could not wait to tell me when he was starting as a writers' agent that Hecht was a client. So, when he asked what kind of film I'd write, if I ever did, I just blurted out the premise."

But I wanted to go back to the topic of writing because there are writers who have tried for years to write professionally but those gatekeepers managed to keep them from realizing that very dream. And then there is John who was more interested in being the next Jack Paar and yet getting an offer to write for a top producer that he turned down. And there were other opportunities that came his way.

When John was a mail boy in the mid-50s at Paramount (and in this country illegally) his closest friend at the studio was Angelo. Angelo was about 30 years old and the son of a successful Greek baker in Chicago who wanted Angelo to follow in his footsteps. Instead, Angelo ran away to Hollywood to be a producer.

"Oh, his father cursed and belittled him, saying he'd fail," John said. "But Angelo heard of a Greek kid named Andrew Fenady[41] who was signed to a deal after making his own low-budget film and he wanted me to write one. I told him I knew nothing about writing movies. I just watched them. Besides, I was only 22 years old at the time. I also told him as low budget, his file could have no sets or lights. It would have to be outdoors, and probably a western."

I interrupted, "That doesn't sound too auspicious."

"It wasn't!" John exclaimed. "But he begged me to try and would give me $500.00. At the time, I had nothing else going on so I tried, never having written a script before. A week later I handed him a western called *The Sun Sets in Hell*. The action took place all in one day. A botched robbery in the morning, and a trick ending at night. Somehow he got the script to Lindsley Parsons[42] who was Allied Artists leading producer of Westerns. Ten days later, Angelo and I were in Parson's office with actor Barry Sullivan[43] and cameraman Haskell Wexler[44] to make a movie."

I had to stop John from talking for a minute just then and absorb what he was telling me. How is it that a kid of just 22 years old, here in the states illegally, who had little interest in writing was sitting in front of such powerhouses? For those who aren't familiar with Wexler, he was the cinematographer for Mike Nichols' *Who's Afraid of Virginia Woolf* and won an Academy Award for it and then went on to be the cinematographer for *In the Heat of the Night*, which starred the aforementioned Sidney Poitier from *Lilies of the Field*. But when John was sitting in front of him then, Wexler, the son of the founder of Allied Radio in Chicago, was just trying to get into the Guild so he hadn't yet quite reached the powerhouse status. I asked John what happened then.

"Well, Sullivan wanted to become a director and the two of them loved my script. It would be their first project. But, the day we were to sign the contract, Allied announced it was no longer making Westerns. And that was that."

"That was that? You must've been heartbroken!"

"Not at all. I was still stunned from even having a meeting. Making a movie meant nothing to me, but I felt bad for Angelo. He was crushed. More so when his father came and dragged him back to the bakery."

"So, I guess that was the end of your movie-script writing then," I said.

"Not quite. Eventually Haskell called. He said he just bought a book for the rights to make a movie. He said I was the only one he thought could write the kind of dialogue and invited me to his white mansion in the Hollywood Hills above the Hollywood Bowl."

"What was the book?"

"*A Long Day in a Short Life* written by Albert Maltz[45]."

"Should I know who that is?"

"Everyone should," John said. "He was one of the blacklisted writers sent to prison for not answering to The House Un-American Activities Committee. I explained I wasn't the right person for the job since I didn't know what a blacklist or Commie was. Haskell just laughed and thought my innocence would bring a nonbiased freshness to the story. He begged me to try it for $600.00 a week for six to ten weeks. And minimum once it was made. But I had a question for him."

"What was the question?"

"Why would he try to make such a film? He glowed and said Frank Sinatra was going to break the blacklist. He was making *The Execution of Private Slovik* at Columbia. It was William Bradford Huie's book about the only American shot for desertion during the Second World War. Dalton Trumbo[46] was hired to do the screenplay. Haskell said that Maltz's book would be hot, so he bought it. I finished the script in six weeks and he was thrilled."

I was impressed that John was in the same company, so to speak, as Dalton Trumbo and hadn't had any writing credits he could yet claim. Not only that, but since he was Canadian he knew little about American politics or screenwriting. I asked John what he thought of what was happening to him.

"It was as unbelievable to me as half the movies I saw as a kid. It never sank in. Even when it got more unbelievable."

"What do you mean?" I said.

"Haskell called me all excited from the set of MGM where he was working. He said there'd be a principal cast reading at his house, which included Richard Widmark.[47] Carol, this overwhelmed me. One of my favorite scenes in a film ever was in Ben Hecht's *Kiss of Death* when Widmark as Tommy Udo cackles while pushing an old lady in a wheelchair down the stairs because she didn't know an ex-con's whereabouts played by Victor Mature.[48] I didn't know how I'd behave meeting him."

"Wow, so do tell us. Were you gushing when you met him?"

"No, because we never met."

"Why?"

"Sinatra canceled his film at Columbia after being accused of being a communist sympathizer at a time when he was campaigning for John F. Kennedy as president. It would hurt Kennedy's chances so Sinatra pulled out of it. Therefore, Haskell canceled his project. I told him Maltz's story had nothing to do with Sinatra and it could be shot low budget in Chicago where he knew everyone, but he declined."

"Did your paths ever cross again with Haskell?"

"Sure. Haskell became my supportive, encouraging best friend for some reason. He asked me to house-sit for him, his wife and his son for a few weeks while he went to Recife in South America to make a documentary about poor farm workers."

"That must've been something," I said, "to stay in such luxury compared to the way you grew up."

John laughed. "Haskell was the most intelligent, well-read person I'd ever met. He had the greatest library of books about Communism, Karl Marx, and so on, West of Moscow. I feasted on those books. I read nearly one a day."

"That explains a lot."

"What do you mean?"

"Why even though you didn't have a formal education, you took advantage of what you had access to."

John nodded. "I must say, to learn what I learned was as thrilling and exciting and mind-expanding as any of the few great films I'd seen. When Haskell returned, he vowed he'd find something we could work on together."

I interrupted John. "You obviously impressed him."

"But I told him I first needed to make a trip," John replied.

"A trip? Where?"

"See, I so loved his family and it made me start to think about the one I didn't have, a father who refused to come back home after the war. I told Haskell I was off to England and Scotland to try and track down my father. Haskell asked me to write him every day. I did. Those letters about the ordeal of meeting my successful father and our parting led to my writing my fourth and final film script for Haskell.

"He asked me to write to him about my background. I really didn't want to, but he had an affinity for minorities, migrant workers and underdogs like me. For a while, anyway. I guess he liked what those letters said because when I got back from finding my father, a story I tell in *Your Mother's Not a Virgin*, Haskell gave me his office at KTTV, his secretary and $600 a week to write about the summer when I was 12. My mother had sent me to a boarding farm in Northern Ontario so that she could be alone with the 'uncles' who came to the house to bed, beat and booze with her. She wanted me out of the way."

John shares this story in detail in his memoir.

"While on this farm," John continued, "two brothers, their cocker spaniel and I, wearing only bathing suits—well, the dog wasn't. Anyway, we ended up getting lost for two days in a bear-infested forest. This one, Carol, I did enjoy writing. Everything was as clear, cruel and fresh as the day it had happened. Reliving it never bothered me. It was like watching a good film. Almost every day for six weeks that it took to finish the story, he'd call after reading the daily pages saying how he loved the dark reality of it and that there'd been no American movie ever about the real domestic violence. It was called simply, *A Summer Thing*. My favorite part was the ending."

"Which was?"

"I am on a train by myself to the United States. It was Haskell's least favorite part. He called me on the phone and said the ending looked like an upbeat Disney movie."

"Really?"

"I told him to show me a Disney film with an hour of domestic violence. He said the ending should hint at darkness. I disagreed and said the story was my story about me. I made it here. I am upbeat."

For anyone who knows John and knows the shoddy treatment he got as a young boy and the hard knocks he got as a young man but sees how he never let those things get him down knows he's not lying. He is always upbeat! I asked John what Haskell's response was.

"He said he wanted to think it over for a few days. Right then, like the Maltz script, I knew it was over. I told him he didn't have to think it over for a few days, adding, 'I know how to make it darker right now.' He asked how. I said, 'We'll make the kid Black!' There was a long silence then the click of the phone. He hung up and never spoke to me again. Even after I became a star 20 years later."

"That makes me sad that he cut you off just like that," I said.

"But his son, Mark" John said, "called to say how much he enjoyed my visits when he was a kid."

"But I'm sure you saw *Bound for Glory* when it came out years later and you were a critic. Since Haskell was involved in the making of that movie, what were your feelings about it?"

"It was a great film in which I said there should be some Oscars, especially for cinematography. Carol, I was reviewing his work, not his character. I can easily separate my feelings about someone's work. With that thought, I was no fan of an often stoned Oliver Stone[49] when they made *Midnight Express* but the last thing I said in my review was that the script deserved an Oscar. And he got it."

I still find it confounding that John doesn't consider himself a writer. Maybe he cannot or doesn't want to write fiction, but that's not to say he's not a writer. All one needs to do is read his reviews, memoir or even daily posts on Facebook and see that the man certainly can turn a witty phrase. But like many others, I'm not the only one who appreciates John's words.

When John's memoir was published, Ed Komenda, a reporter for *Reno Gazette-Journal* and *USA Today*, spent six hours at John's house interviewing him. Ed also called John's son, Christopher Barbour, who was co-executive producer of the smash series *Criminal Minds*, to ask him what he remembered most about his father. John was certain Chris would recall the times John took him to participate in golf tournaments, to the movies or meeting celebrities. Instead, Chris said, "I remember and miss the clacking sound of his typewriter."

"Carol," John said, "it moved me to tears. Almost like poetry. And what was I typing then? Those reviews."

Notes

1 https://en.wikipedia.org/wiki/Sidney_Poitier
2https://www.newyorker.com/magazine/1939/08/19/the-wizard-of-hollywood
3 https://en.wikipedia.org/wiki/Broderick_Crawford
4 https://en.wikipedia.org/wiki/Robert_Donat
5 https://en.wikipedia.org/wiki/O._Henry
6 https://en.wikipedia.org/wiki/Mark_Twain
7 https://en.wikipedia.org/wiki/W._Somerset_Maugham
8 https://en.wikipedia.org/wiki/Guy_de_Maupassant
9 https://en.wikipedia.org/wiki/Upton_Sinclair
10 https://en.wikipedia.org/wiki/Jack_Paar
11 https://en.wikipedia.org/wiki/Edward_R._Murrow
12 https://en.wikipedia.org/wiki/Lenny_Bruce
13 https://en.wikipedia.org/wiki/Jonathan_Winters
14 https://en.wikipedia.org/wiki/Mario_Machado
15 http://www.bradlachman.com/
16 https://en.wikipedia.org/wiki/FCC_fairness_doctrine
17 https://en.wikipedia.org/wiki/Jim_Garrison
18https://www.latimes.com/local/obituaries/la-me-geoff-miller-20110418-story.html
19 https://en.wikipedia.org/wiki/Burt_Prelutsky
20 https://en.wikipedia.org/wiki/Merv_Griffin
21 https://en.wikipedia.org/wiki/David_Frost
22 https://en.wikipedia.org/wiki/Joe_Pyne
23 https://en.wikipedia.org/wiki/Redd_Foxx
24https://www.history.com/this-day-in-history/massacre-begins-at-munich-olympics
25 https://en.wikipedia.org/wiki/Johnny_Carson
26 https://en.wikipedia.org/wiki/Neil_Simon
27 https://en.wikipedia.org/wiki/Tom_Brokaw
28 https://en.wikipedia.org/wiki/Paddy_Chayefsky
29 https://en.wikipedia.org/wiki/Peter_Finch
30 https://en.wikipedia.org/wiki/Faye_Dunaway
31 https://en.wikipedia.org/wiki/Beatrice_Straight
32 https://en.wikipedia.org/wiki/Mike_Nichols
33 https://en.wikipedia.org/wiki/Dustin_Hoffman
34 https://en.wikipedia.org/wiki/Anne_Bancroft

35 https://en.wikipedia.org/wiki/Ray_Stark
36 https://en.wikipedia.org/wiki/Ben_Hecht
37 https://en.wikipedia.org/wiki/Warren_Beatty
38 https://en.wikipedia.org/wiki/Frank_Sinatra
39 https://en.wikipedia.org/wiki/Bob_Hope
40 https://en.wikipedia.org/wiki/Burt_Reynolds
41 https://en.wikipedia.org/wiki/Andrew_J._Fenady
42 https://en.wikipedia.org/wiki/Lindsley_Parsons
43 https://en.wikipedia.org/wiki/Barry_Sullivan_(American_actor)
44 https://en.wikipedia.org/wiki/Haskell_Wexler
45 https://en.wikipedia.org/wiki/Albert_Maltz
46 https://en.wikipedia.org/wiki/Dalton_Trumbo
47 https://en.wikipedia.org/wiki/Richard_Widmark
48 https://en.wikipedia.org/wiki/Victor_Mature
49 https://en.wikipedia.org/wiki/Oliver_Stone

II. Raising the Hackles

I've said it before but it bears repeating: John Barbour isn't afraid to tell the truth…or at the very least, his opinion. I thought about this as I was browsing through some of the reviews he'd copied and sent me. One must have confidence, courage or just not give a damn in order to write honest reviews when so many who were part of making those movies—from investors to producers to directors to actors—were all hoping would garner raves. After all, it's their career, which leads me to first share this review John wrote for the movie version of *The Sunshine Boys* released in 1975. Enjoy:

What Sunshine Could Use Is a Little Chicken Soup

By John Barbour

And other old Jewish remedies

Neil Simon has written almost as many successful plays as Harris & Frank[1] have suits; when they are taken off the stage and put on the screen, though, they don't look as good. And the fault is Simon's. The best characters in his plays reflect an ethnic-New-York-Jewish background, and he has captured the distinctive humor and honest of such a background so effectively and entertainingly, he has become one of the world's wealthiest playwrights. But something goes wrong when he moves his characters cross-country to Hollywood.

Maybe it's his wanting them to be more loved outside New York, or maybe it's his desire to get even wealthier. But what he frequently does is water down that original background and the characters—perhaps to make them more digestible to Middle America—thus robbing them of a wonderful uniqueness. It's like trying to turn sour cream and blintzes into mayonnaise and white bread. In the movie version of *Come Blow Your Horn*, Frank Sinatra somehow became the Italian son of Jewish parents; in other films, his Jewish characters became so nondescript they could have been nondenominational WASPs.

Now, *The Sunshine Boys*, about two aging Jewish comedians who worked together for 40 years but couldn't stand each other, was one of Simon's best plays. Onstage, Jack Albertson[2] and Sam Levene[3] were perfect. They and the material came together like lox and bagels. You wouldn't think Simon would want to change this to ham and eggs, but in recasting the film, he has denied it at least partially of some of its delicatessen flavor and tumult. George Burns[4] is cast as one member of the vaudeville team. However, Burns, a revered entertainer, is a nice man—and it unfortunately shows. His over-easy characterization projects none of the underlying hostility which helps provide the comedic spark between him and his partner, played by Walter Matthau[5], who makes up for it by being overly hostile and hammy. Even though he says a lot of funny things, you find yourself liking him only because Richard Benjamin[6], who is wonderful as his nephew and agent, likes him so much. Paradoxically, it's Benjamin's presence as a straight man which makes *The Sunshine Boys* more than just *The Odd Couple* 30 years later.

Neil Simon's plays prove he is an excellent writer; what his movies show, though, is that he is not much of a rewriter or a casting director.

When I read that review, I foolishly kept wondering if John was concerned that he'd upset Neil Simon. After all, by 1966, Simon had four successful productions running on Broadway at the same time. Apparently, John still felt his review was merited. He said, "Even if Shakespeare got royalties, he'd never be as rich as Neil Simon was. Neil did not need a studio to finance his film.

He had the money, and in coming to Hollywood he tried to *Presbytertianize* his original characters, who, as Jews, resembled every man. Instead, he turned them into two humans no one likes or recognizes. I suggested the next thing Neil should write is a letter firing himself as his own casting director."

I wanted to know if John ever got a reaction from Mr. Simon.

"Sure," John said. "I got a phone call and not the first from someone who was responding to my review. This time it was Neil laughing. He said, 'John, 'truth is truth, and funny is funny! By the way, I did like your comedy album, *It's Tough to Be White*, and heard you mention you're doing another one. True?' I said yes. Actually it's based on stuff from my reviews and calling it, *I Met a Man I Didn't Like*. He said, 'Perfect. I knew Will Rogers was a liar. I'd like to do the liner notes.' I said, Wow. To get even? He laughed. 'If I have to!'

"Carol, he and Burt Reynolds[7] and a few other biggies did the liner notes. Not much happened to the album, which is a good album. I think it has the first strong piece about cigarettes and cancer, and Vietnam. But months later Neil called and said, 'John, those liner notes were the least successful writing I ever did!'"

I was impressed that Neil Simon, who passed away in August of 2018, was so good humored about John's critique of his movie but I do know that others in the business didn't respond quite the same way when John reviewed their work.

So it was with the movie *Soylent Green* starring Charlton Heston[8]. As with some of his reviews, this one was brief but packed a punch.

Soylent Green

By John Barbour

Charlton Heston never performs well in any film in which he wears shoes and socks. Judging by the job he does under Richard Fleischer's klutzy direction in this trite film about the effects of overpopulation in 2022, he must be wearing two sizes too small. Chuck Heston and Chuck Connors[9] together add up to chuck the movie.

First, it's stunning to see that futuristic *Soylent Green* was taking place in 2022, just a year from when this book is being written. That aside, I asked John what happened after that review came out.

"First, let me tell you that I added that nobody deliberately makes an awful movie. They are good talented people. They just turn out that way. I said, 'I'd like to say something nice about the film: that the sets were beautiful, but they'd be more beautiful if they'd been placed in front of the actors."

"You certainly don't hold back," I said.

"Well, the producer from Fox thought I was being unfair and wanted to sue me. For five years he went through the LA courts, the California Supreme Court, all the way to DC and the final Supreme Court. But, they turned him down, telling him that John Barbour's reviews are of no public importance."

"Ouch. How did you feel getting a negative review from the court?"

"Funny, but the court was right. What a waste of time. I didn't write reviews for the public. I wrote them for myself. And was accidentally lucky enough to earn a living at it. I never took myself seriously but, thankfully, many did."

"Which leads us back to Charlton Heston," I said.

"Well," John said, "after bombing a different film, *The Omega Man*, Heston called to be a guest on one of my shows to listen to the review in person. At the time I was doing a 90 minute late-night poor man's *Tonight Show* on Saturdays on KNBC. It was here I gave our weekend sportscaster, Bryant Gumbel[10], his first job as a co-host. That clip is somewhere on my website. (Johnbarboursworld.com.) But even bigger than Heston were Burt Reynolds and Neil Simon."

Since we'd already discussed Neil Simon, I asked about Burt Reynolds. I always enjoyed watching him on talk shows, even if I didn't care so much for many of his movies.

John said, "In bombing *White Lightning*, I said Burt was in a position to pick the diamonds of scripts but instead kept choosing zircons like this where writers don't write dialogue, they write car chases. After my review on Friday, my phone rang. It was Burt. Before I barely finished saying hello, he said, 'I'm booking myself on your show tomorrow night.'"

"And anyone who wants to see this interview can see it on your aforementioned website," I said. "I've watched it more than once since it is so entertaining."

John nodded. "It's had over 200k views so far. Anyway, Burt showed up alone. He was the first guest, of course. The interview in which we confronted each other was a 14-minute joy. After I moved on to the next guest, he sat next to Bryant and never left. Later, he told me it was his favorite interview ever."

"That's awesome. But his appearance didn't compromise any of your other reviews of movies he did, even though you did enjoy *The End*...and then his next movie was a disappointment to you. Here's a taste of those reviews for our readers:

Burt Reynolds Breaks Out

By John Barbour

The charm displayed on Carson's couch at last comes through on the big screen...

In almost every one of Burt Reynolds' films to date, his performances have been as plastic as a starlet's chest. In too many movies like *Shamus* and *White Lightning*, all that pseudo-masculine Reynolds *machismo* would give you the giggles, because it looked like such a put-on. But if appearances in films convinced you he was a lousy actor, his appearances on TV talk shows convinced you he was a fantastic Burt Reynolds.

If his movie portrayals seemed stilted, it was because under that manufactured, grim-jawed exterior was a grinning interior. Reynolds possesses a sense of humor and a self-deprecating charm on Johnny Carson's couch that somehow gets smaller on the big screen.

In his latest film, though, *The Longest Yard*, the only mask he wears is the one on his football helmet, and for the first time we see not only the complete and easy personality, we see the talent, too; now we won't have Burt Reynolds, the non-actor, to kick around anymore.

Reynolds plays an ex-professional football player whose girlfriend calls the police because he takes her car after leaving the bedroom where he was too tired to take *her*. After fouling one of the arresting officers with a knee, he is sentenced to two years in a state prison.

The guards there have a football team which is the all-consuming passion of Warden Eddie Albert[11], who's excellent as a combination of Vince Lombardi[12] and Captain Queeg[13] with a machine gun. To help prepare the guards' team for their upcoming season and to avoid further punishment, Reynolds agrees to quarterback a team made up of prisoners. Some of the most entertaining moments in this very entertaining film occur when he selects the players from among the inmates. His first draft choices are axe-murderers, black militants, and one incredibly dumb giant who talks as though he does push-ups with his tongue. Together they devise such plays as inflicting incidental punishment after the whistle blows. The game itself lasts almost 45 minutes, and the audience cheers for Burt's Mean Machine as though they were the Rams in the Superbowl.

Produced by Al Ruddy[14] (of *Godfather* fame), very well-directed by Robert Aldrich[15], and wittily scripted by Tracy Keenan Wynn[16], *The Longest Yard*, in spite of a couple of slightly hokey, predictable moments, is almost perfect film entertainment. You might call it a movie massage: you know you're being manipulated, but you like the way it feels.

And then there's Smokey and the Bandit:

If the heavily publicized restaurant Burt Reynolds opened in Atlanta had as little thought put into it as some of his recent movies have then it should be closed by the health department. Reynolds, who has proven he is a charming and capable actor, seems to have given up trying to make movies that are movies and instead makes ones that are more like cartoons. At its best, his current *Smokey and the Bandit* is a Road Runner cartoon, with Burt as a character somewhere between the Road Runner and Bugs Bunny, and Jackie Gleason[17] as Wiley Coyote. It's a 90-minute chase scene. And at its worst, which is most of the time, it's designed for people with transmissions for brains.

Burt plays a legendary driver known from Texarkana to Yazoo by his

CB handle "Bandit." His partner is Jerry Reed[18]. They are hired by Pat McCormack[19] and Paul Williams[20] to drive 900 miles, pick up 400 cases of Coors beer, illegally transport it cross-country and be back in 28 hours. Williams and McCormack, as a wealthy father and son with more money than brains, are the greatest mismatch since Eddie Fisher[21] and Liz Taylor[22]; if they had only $8 between them they'd have more money than brains. Williams' part is beneath him—and you know how tall *he* is.

Anyway, Burt drives a souped-up Firebird as a lead car, which ends up cleaner than when it started, and Jerry Reed drives a big semi—accompanied by a semi-big dog. They pick up beer, and Burt picks up Sally Field[23] hitchhiking in a wedding gown—unfortunately, though, the goon she left at the altar is Sheriff Jackie Gleason's son, and Gleason's not going to let any dame embarrass him or his dumb kin. So he takes off in pursuit of the unsuspecting Reynolds.

Gleason is perfect for the role because he's at least louder than the trucks. The only honest line in the film is when Gleason says, "What we have here is disrespect for the law!" All the police come across with the mentality of dip sticks. Burt's best moment is his one-line Gabby Hayes[24] impression. And Reed is an excellent actor who could go far in films—the further he goes from films like this.

But the most depressing thing in the film is that the night I saw it, half the people in the audience who were whooping and hollering and talking to the screen were of voter age. In going 1800 miles at 120 mph, Burt stopped only once for gas—that's 90 miles to a gallon. So if you believe that any American car gets 90 miles to a gallon, then you'll believe *Smokey and the Bandit* is worthwhile.

Great News! Burt Reynolds' Career May Not Be Terminal

See? Everything works out in "The End"

During the past few weeks, Burt Reynolds has made more TV appearances than Mrs. Olson[25]. Half the time he's been selling a movie called *The End.* The other half he's been telling critics they can kiss it. In much the same way Nixon[26] keeps protesting his innocence, Reynolds keeps protesting to Merv (Griffin) and Mike (Douglas)[27] and Dinah (Shore)[28] and Johnny (Carson) that critics don't mean anything. On one of these shows, he said that he has never lied to the public about what to expect from films like *White Lightning, Gator* and *Semi-Tough*. Why then should he expect critics to?

If I were Reynolds and I had made *Smokey and the Bandit*, which was little more than a Roadrunner cartoon, I wouldn't listen to what the critics had to say, either. I'd listen to my accountant. As an old Spanish proverb, and an Italian singer from Hoboken say, "The good life is the best revenge!"

If Reynolds is looking for the good life *and* revenge, he will get both from *The End.* And if he's looking to dump on critics he'd better get it out of his system *now*, because after all the reviews are in he won't have them to kick around anymore. Because there won't be that many who won't love the film.

The End is the best thing Reynolds has ever done, either as an actor or a director. There are some individual scenes in it, written by Jerry Belson,[29] that are as bright and sharp and funny as those of any comedy to come out of Hollywood since Reynolds told Darren McGavin[30] where he could shove *Riverboat*.

Our star plays a TV real-estate salesman who is told that God is about to foreclose on him. Over the opening credits we hear him talking to a nurse who is preparing him for a urinalysis. It's like a good radio show, and the audience starts to giggle. It's a perfect setup for the movie—and for Reynolds' first line on camera. When we finally see him he is standing forlornly in the doctor's office. He says, "I have the same thing Ali MacGraw[31] had in *Love Story*."

He goes on to tell the doctor he didn't know he was sick, he just thought he'd found a new way of losing weight: throwing up. When he leaves the doctor's office, depressed, the first thing he sees is a funeral cortege, which he follows to the graveyard; and as he sits in his car contemplating his future, we see the shadow of the crucifix on the church steeple outlined on his forehead. It's a terrific touch.

Because so much in *The End* is so good, the flaws can be forgiven. In the second half, Dom DeLuise's[32] presence seems to overwhelm Reynolds and from here on the film at times takes on a frantic, slapstick broadness that had earlier been avoided.

The same year that *The End* was released, so was *Hooper*, starring, of course, Burt Reynolds. Here's what John had to say about that:

I wish Burt Reynolds would take a rest. So I could. It seems he has a movie coming out once a month. A couple of months ago I devoted three pages to him and *The End*; I figured he deserved three pages because for me it was the longest wait from *The Longest Yard* till I found something with Reynolds I liked. After that review I swore I wasn't going to mention his name for two issues—I was beginning to see his name in this column more often than mine. Unfortunately, I made this promise before I saw *Hooper*. It seems as soon as Reynolds does something good, he has a compulsion to immediately revert to something terrible. He started out in show business as a stunt man. A few more movies like *Hooper*, and he may end up as one.

In *Hooper*, Reynolds plays the greatest stunt man in movies, whose reputation is as big and as legendary as the Hollywood sign. And like the Hollywood sign, he is aging and falling apart and is about to be replaced by a newer one—obviously an affectionate tribute by Reynolds to this unique breed of performer, and to his own past.

The trouble with *Hooper*, though, is that while Reynolds and his buddies are having a ball brawling and boozing, they don't let the audience in on it. It's as though we are forced to watch someone else's private party. But what's worse is that for the first hour all we see are a series of stunts that aren't any more interesting than those we could see on the Universal Tour, when we should be getting some insight into the people who execute them. The plot and characters are thinner and phonier than the fake glass they fall through.

In an attempt to show what's going on in Reynold's mind, there are a couple of scenes where he gets out of bed at night and stands in front of the mirror in his jockey shorts looking at the scars on his body. He looks at the stitches, in fact, like notches in the pistol of a gunslinger who's running out of bullets—and time. And like the aging gunslinger, he becomes a little more concerned when he hears there's a new guy in town who's younger and better. This is the kind of premise Sid Caesar[33] could have made a great skit out of, but it's not enough for a movie.

In *Hooper*, we are supposed to get the impression movies cannot be made without stunt men. Burt Reynolds has it confused. Movies can be made without stunt men—but not without writers.

As it happens and to John's shock, his wife, Sarita, recalled that Burt and John had exchanged letters. Sarita managed to find those letters and so we thought it would be fun to share them here with you. Enjoy!

Burt Reynolds

John—

What a shame when someone you really think is bright and witty and sometimes quite caustically brilliant says your acting is "more wooden than a Georgia forest!" I would quit acting all together, but I have also read "Time" magazine and "Saturday Review" (you must read them sometime) and they just adore my 'hairy' little body!

As for the staple remark, it's a cheap joke I used on the "Tonight" Show over four months ago.

But I will continue to give you material, - I once used one of your lenses on the same show - so we're even.

Gosh, I hope you like me someday, but will that mean that all really respected reviewers won't?!

Warmly yours
Burt

MM 11
KTTV
METROMEDIA TELEVISION
5746 SUNSET BOULEVARD
LOS ANGELES, CALIFORNIA 90028
(213) 462-7111

Sept. 13/72.

John Barbour.

Burt:

In your earlier struggles as an actor, when you got bombed by some reviewer, I'm sure your agents and press agents and friends would say to you, "what do reviewers know!" If you got good reviews in "Time" and "Saturday Review" for "Deliverance" just remember, "what do reviewers know!"

I have met some of those reviewers who write for some of those Eastern Periodicals. They dictate their pieces to secretaries, because if they weild a pencil or type for more than fifteen seconds, they tire their already limp wrists. They would love you no matter what you did because they are turned on by any dark man who looks like he trims his hairy little body with a lawnmower. As frustrated hair-dressers, they would just adore jumping on you and braiding your chest.

Burt, I really first became aware of you a couple of years ago when I was hosting an early morning show on ABC here in Los Angeles. I had seen you in "Hawk" and years earlier in "Riverboat". As an actor at the time I thought your range of emotion consisted of two surly expressions: one with yours eyes open, and one with your eyes closed. But then I picked up a copy of one of the Trades in which you did an interview expressing how you thought you had been misused in this town as an actor, that you felt you never had a chance to show that side of you which was witty and warm and charming and otherwise delightful. At first I thought, is he kidding; I thought if he had twice the wit and charm he has already shown he still wouldn't come off as warm as Jack La Rue.

Then I saw you on the Tonight Show..and Dinah's Place. And indeed you were delightful. And indeed you had been misused. And that moment on the Tonight Show between you and Judy was one of the most entertaining and electric in the history of that show. What wasn't said was funnier than all the great spoken jokes on that program..including the one you stole from me.

(cont'd.)

(2)

What impressed me the most was the fact as an actor you couldn't have had it too easy, and yet you were able to convert that hostility and disappointment into a fuel that forged in you a greater sense of awareness in your identity. When the opportunity to express that identity came on those talk shows, it came across as witty and warm and charming and deceptively intelligent. And you were right in saying what you said about yourself a couple of years earlier. First, probabl because no one else would say it for you, and, secondly, why should Lee Trevino say he is a five handicap golfer when all the time he knows he's sub par.

The trick now is to capture that essence as an actor. "Colombo" is an extension of Peter Falk, Don Corlioni was an extension of Marlon Brando, and no matter what Cary Grant did, it was always an extension of Cary Grant. What you do as an actor must, to really be effective, be an extension of you. You have all the ingredients to be as good as anyone, but for some reason or other, be it choice of material, choice of Director, or something in you, you haven't really let it happen...but I'm sure you will.

In the meantime, until such a time as I get to do my own stuff on the Tonight Show, I will also continue to provide you with material, because unlike Henny Youngman you know how to take just the good stuff...maybe that's why you've only used one line so far.

Also, I am earning more money selling Xerox copies of your letter to the women in my family than I am as a reviewer. Thanks for helping to augment my income. And thanks for taking the time out to write that brilliant put-down...because the truth is if I wasn't good, you wouldn't have bothered, and you must also know by now that your name in the business is magic and people think I have been covered with gold just because you went out of your way to shit on me.

Keep up the good work which comes from being Burt Reynolds.

Warmest Regards,

[signature]

When one thinks of Alfred Hitchcock[34], one cannot help but think of some of his classics, including *The Birds, Psycho, North by Northwest, Dial M for Murder, Rear Window* and dozens of others. I have a friend who was so traumatized by *The Birds*, having watched it as a child, that to this day, she freaks out if a bird is anywhere near her. For me, *Rear Window* was and is much more disturbing, since to me, it is more realistic. Besides, it was easy for me to root for Jimmy Stewart[35] as he is stuck in that wheelchair.

Turner Classic Movies often airs Hitchcock films, films that garnered 46 Academy Award nominations, receiving six wins, however, Hitchcock never won for Best Director even though he had five nominations. One of the last films that Hitchcock made was *Frenzy* in 1972.

In ink, John wrote,

Alfred Hitchcock's comeback, while not a total triumph, is diverting throughout. Unfortunately, though, the suspense is little more than lukewarm by the time the climax rolls around and we're never as surprised as we expect to be. Jon Finch is a surly, down-on-his luck Londoner who, on top of everything else, is mistaken by Scotland Yard for a psychotic tie-murderer. By the time he's convicted and sent up, he's really fit to be tied. Hitchcock is not a director, he's a confectioner: making 32 flavors of the same spooky theme.

The very idea of insulting Hitchcock, who always seemed creepy to me, made me think that he could cause great harm to that critic who didn't rave about his film. I asked John if there were any repercussions; you know, like being chased by a crop duster plane or having an assassin put his sites on him?

John laughed and then said, "Believe it or not, at his 50th year anniversary party at a plush Beverly Hills restaurant, with every star imaginable there, he came over to my table and gave me a mug with his picture and said, 'Young man, I sell a lot of ice cream movies.' And I still have that mug. It's next to the one with Jim Garrison.[36]" (Anyone familiar with John's writing and videos, knows the relationship he had with Jim Garrison.)

Admittedly, there are movies that were crucified by the critics that I loved. And there were movies that the critics raved about that made me scratch my head and wonder if it was me or just the fact that our tastes were different. But, there is something entertaining when reading a writer as witty as John is where he uses words to destroy a movie's chances at the box office. Okay, that may be a bit of an exaggeration and actually mean-spirited on my part, but John was hired to tell viewers what to expect when going to the movies and if he were to love every movie, he would lose credibility. (Don't worry, readers, I'll be sharing favorable reviews but beware they quite likely won't make you laugh out loud as much as the unfavorable reviews.)

Now, buckle up. We're moving on to our next one.

Ali MacGraw and Steve McQueen

Let's 'Getaway' from it All

Sam Peckinpah[37] is the Hugh Hefner[38] of homicide. A closet sadist masquerading as a moralist, he makes celluloid comic strips for the emotionally handicapped. The sad thing is, as in the case of *The Getaway*, his films move with a kind of energy and vitality which temporarily takes your mind off the fact that there are more holes in the story than in some of the corpses. Which is almost like saying that with this Steve McQueen[39]-Ali MacGraw starrer there is good news and there is bad news. The good news is that it may make money. The bad news is that it may make money.

After spending four years in prison, McQueen is sprung by a crooked politician who has spent those four years with Steve's wife (Ali), the understanding being that once out, Steve will help pull off a half-million dollar bank robbery.

After a few double crosses and a few corpses, he is left holding the money and Ali, and since there is really no one left with whom to split the loot, there is no reason for him to go to the pre-arranged meeting spot near the Mexican border. Peckinpah ignores the fact that this is where his story falls apart, and hopes the audience will do the same if a few more bodies and cars fall apart.

In making a film about a character who gets away with robbery and murder, Peckinpah may feel that he is making a film about the American fantasy. When he was a younger man sitting in theatres engrossed in those Warner Brothers' gangster films of the '30s and '40s, he, like most of his contemporaries, probably found himself rooting for the bad guys—Cagney[40], Bogart[41], Robinson[42], *et al.* And when they were gunned down or caught with the loot by the good guys just 30 seconds before the end, he probably also thought about what they should have done in order to make a getaway.

So when Peckinpah grew up, or rather when he got older, what *he* did in order to get away with it was to make a movie. For the bad guys to succeed, he reasoned, you don't have bad guys vs. bad guys. *The Godfather* was of the same genre, but in *The Getaway*, instead of remembering the characters, you remember only the cadavers.

Steve McQueen plays Bullitt again. Sally Struthers[43], as a frumpy little housewife who becomes enamored of the gunman who abducts her, displays an ability to whine that, with practice, could make her the screen's next Shelley Winters[44].

As for Ali MacGraw, who has the most doe-ful eyes since Bambi, her reading of lines indicates that in her recent marital rift, she obviously didn't get custody of the dialogue coach.

"John," I said, "you mention Peckinpah and his short comings several times in this review."

"Well, for me, it only had one good scene in it and when I reviewed it on air, I said, 'To compliment this film for just one good scene is like complimenting Tijuana for the one good toilet that flushes.'"

"Yikes."

"Yikes is right," John said. "I'd have to say that this was the only physically dangerous review I did. When I got back to my little office, the phone was ringing. I picked it up and a drunken Peckinpah was screaming, 'you asshole! I'm gonna cut your fuckin' head off and piss down your throat.' When I tried to explain that his film was far away from his TV series with Brian Keith[45], *The Westerner*. The best western ever on TV. But he didn't listen. Instead, he screamed, 'you're a dead man!' and hung up."

"Well, since I'm talking to you, I'm guessing nothing came of that threat, but did he scare you?"

"Not at all. The only time I was concerned is when someone shot bullets through the windshield of my classic Studebaker following my review of the Jerry Lewis[46] telethon. KNBC had to hire an extra security guard. But that was a TV show."

For anyone not familiar with the telethon, let me explain. Its full name was The Jerry Lewis MDA Labor Day Telethon[47] and aired annually for 21½ hours, starting on the Sunday night prior to Labor Day and continuing until late Monday afternoon. It began in 1966 and ended 2011. Jerry would have entertainment and introduce viewers to those with Muscular Dystrophy, all in an attempt to raise funds for the cause.

So, I asked John what he said to cause such a violent reaction.

"Well, I bombed Jerry Lewis for his telethon. I got offended when I watched it and Jerry said he was there "to correct God's mistakes." That is an actual quote of his. I said, "Jesus Christ!" He was an egomaniac. Anyway, I went on the air and said, 'You know, it used to be called the Muscular Dystrophy Telethon. Now they call it the Jerry Lewis Telethon. That's because someday they expect to find a cure for Muscular Dystrophy, but they'll never find a cure for Jerry Lewis." The crew laughed. I brought up the quote about God's mistake. I said, 'You know, they raised twenty-three million dollars, but maybe they could raise twice that amount from every man, woman and child that never wanted to see him again if they donated a quarter.

"Well, my God, the switchboard lit up. They had to hire a couple of guards. They kicked me out of the building at one point. The reason they could fire me, which they did three times, was because I never had a contract. Then the general manager of the station called me and said, 'Nobody would have the balls to tell the truth the way you just did. You're coming back.' I came back and decided to read three or four pieces of vitriolic hate mail directed to me. I went on air and read the scathing hate mail."

I remembered Labor Day weekends watching the telethon but as the years went by, I found Jerry Lewis to be, well, less funny and more obnoxious. He was the comedian who made me laugh when watching *The Nutty Professor* and *Cinderfella* so it saddened me to see just how arrogant he came across. Correct God's mistakes? I don't blame John for weighing in on this. Yet, it just goes to show how people can't handle the truth as Jack Nicholson[48] said in *A Few Good Men*.

So now we're moving on to *The Great Gatsby*. The book by F. Scott Fitzgerald, which was required reading for me in high school, has been brought to the big screen four times over the last seventy years or so. The first, in 1949, starred Alan Ladd[49] as Gatsby himself, which I've never seen. Another attempt that I never saw was made in 2000 with an English actor as Gatsby named Toby Stephens[50]. Paul Rudd[51] was Carraway and Mira Sorvino[52], Daisy. The most recent one, 2013, which was a musical starred Leonardo DiCaprio[53], Tobey Maguire[54] as Carraway, and directed by Baz Luhrmann[55]. I'm guessing John will be appalled with me since I thoroughly enjoyed that version and I suppose it's because I enjoyed the soundtrack so much, being a fan of Florence + the Machine, Beyonce, Fergie and others. I tend to blast the CD when driving in my car. (Yes, I still have CDs!) If I recall, too, there was the option of watching that particular *Gatsby* with 3-D glasses. I opted not to.

But now I'm going to go back to the 1974 version, which is the one John reviewed and created more problems for himself since he raised some more hackles. He told me, "Carol, it cost just $3 to see any movie. The president of Paramount, Phyllis Diller, his real name is Barry[56], but I call him Phyllis, was so proud of this film, saying it would be Paramount's biggest grosser ever, that he intended to double the admission to $6. They spent millions in advertising it. It was on the covers of *Time* and *Newsweek*. There were billboards and Gatsby parties all over town. Diller said they'd also make millions from the Gatsby clothing line they were putting out. The film was awful. And I said the only way Diller could get $6 was to charge $3 to get in and $3 to get out. The quote lived and the movie died.

Great Gatsby? Better a Great Chase

By John Barbour

"Whenever a movie gets a big publicity hype, chances are it's a dog, like *Catch-22* or *Lost Horizon…*"

Hopefully this will be the last review you will have to read about *The Great Gatsby*, even though for a long time yet we may still be hearing Ali McGraw's last laugh.

A few days before Gatsby opened, I had occasion to be the first to review it, a review that was seen on KNBC's *Six O'clock News* and resulted in Paramount's repossessing my screening invitations. Anyway, those first thoughts I had about The Making of The Great Gatsby now turn out to be fairly Universal. (Which is another studio that once rescinded my invitations.)

Whenever a movie is given a huge pre-release publicity hype the chances are it's a dog. *Catch-22* got a pre-release cover story in *Time*; then it was lucky to catch 22 customers. Similar hypes were given to *Lost Horizon* and *Jonathan Livingston Seagull.* With all the advance promo given *Gatsby*, I couldn't tell if Paramount's Bob Evans[57] was making a movie or going back into the clothing business.

If it's true that the bigger the hype the bigger the dog, then *Gatsby* is a St. Bernard. The studio spent a fortune recapturing F. Scott Fitzgerald's period, but lost Fitzgerald's generation. Robert Redford[58] plays the mysterious millionaire who throws huge parties at his mansion with all the pizazz of Hugh Hefner. Although he had to speak dialogue that even Olivier[59] would find tough to make believable, Redford would have to improve to be dull. As lovers, he and Mia Farrow[60] couldn't make sparks together rubbing their feet on a new carpet.

Director Jack Clayton's[61] slow film philosophy is that a thousand pictures are worth one word, so all we look at endlessly are beautiful close-ups of Mia's sparkling eyes and hair; it's like a 2 ½ hour Breck commercial. The one good thing about Gatsby is that it may once and for all put an end to nostalgia.

I wasn't sure what John meant regarding Ali McGraw's last laugh so I did some internet research. Apparently, Ali was desperate to play Daisy Buchanan but didn't get or take the role; depends on which story you believe.

Anyway, John said, "After that review, Diller, like others, tried unsuccessfully to get me fired. After I lost *Real People*[62] for trying to tell Jim Garrison's story, I created an even better concept, a show called *Reliable Sources*. I say it was a better concept because I was going to do real news. To co-host it,

I hired a young guy named Greg Kinnear[63] after seeing him on something called *Talk Soup*. I did the pilot for Greg Nathanson, the GM at Fox's KTTV, which was part of their growing network. But wouldn't you know it: Diller was the president. Nathanson loved the show and believed me when I said Kinnear could become the biggest star in TV, but Diller said, 'No way.' As we all know, Kinnear went on to make it in the movies instead."

Reading the dozens upon dozens of reviews that John sent me from those magazines he'd found in his trunk is nothing but entertaining. His writing seems effortless so I asked him if there was a movie he'd found difficult to review.

He replied, "There were two. The first was *Death Race 2000*. Believe it or not, when my son, Christopher, was five or six, I took him to a lot of the movies. Even R rated ones. I just loved being with him. So I took him to see *Death Race 2000*. The movie opens with doctors and nurses wheeling sick and dying patients out onto the freeway and betting on who gets run over first. Christopher told me that he couldn't watch it, but I told him I had to because it was my job. He replied that he'd wait in the lobby for me then. I said to him, 'You're kidding. An hour and an half of you sitting alone out there. No way.' He responded that there was no way he was sitting there with his eyes shut the whole time, adding 'I can still hear the screams.' That's when I told him we'd go home and we got up and left."

"So, then you didn't review that movie?" I said.

"Carol," John said, "what I just told you is how I reviewed it on the air and in print."

"Wow," I said, wanting to get Christopher's memory on those movie outings with his father. So John invited me to reach out to Christopher, which I did.

"Oh, yes, he did," Christopher confirmed. "Dad always brought me along. We went to Fox Theater in Hollywood."

I asked Christopher if he recalled any of those particular movies. "Sure. *Who'll Stop the Rain* for one. It starred Nick Nolte and was an R rated war movie. Another movie he took me to was *Five Fingers of Death*, which was the beginning of the invasion of martial arts films."

I found it interesting that John brought his young child to such films. My kids, all adults now, would tell you how I tried to keep them from seeing violent or frightening movies when they were young. Maybe I was being overprotective. Who knows, but Chris didn't feel he was harmed in any way by seeing such movies, although he did walk out of *Aliens* since that was too frightening for him. "I also didn't like to see people kissing," he added. "And we went to a lot of foreign movies. One in particular was with a young boy eager to see an adult woman naked. You could never get away with a movie like that today," he said. "There was also the time we took a friend of mine to the movies. We were about ten or eleven years old. Dad was going to review *Raging Bull*. My friend started to cry while we were in the lobby, saying that his parents would be upset because he wasn't allowed to watch movies like that. So my dad called his mom to get permission, which he got."

"So did you find that you and your father had similar tastes?" I asked.

"Not always," Chris said. "The first movie I recall that we disagreed on was *Star Wars*. Dad didn't like it, but I loved it."

I got John's memory on this:

"I viewed it (Star Wars) as a comic book, but a successful one that would be a franchise. I was more than right. Also, it is also the first time a movie critic, not too fond of the film himself, suggested people buy 20th Century stock from the company that made it. I was dead-on there too. Also, three days later, I bought rubber head masks of the leading characters for Christopher. We still have them. Worth a small fortune!"

I'm guessing Chris is around the same age as my son, who also loved *Star Wars* and could have watched it repeatedly, but it appears that Chris may have forgotten, or just been too young to recall when he and his father disagreed on an earlier film that was released in 1972. Here's what John wrote in this particular review:

I took my wife and three year old son to see *Alice's Adventures in Wonderland* on a Saturday afternoon. My son has a fairly sophisticated taste for a boy who still wears Pampers and sleeps with a four foot frog. He loves Tom Jones[64], Redd Foxx, *Dragnet, Wonderama*, and he doesn't tell people I used to work at Channel Eleven; he tells them I used to work with Fred Flintstone. He likes the Flintstones because he thinks they're more adult than Doris Day[65]. Well, he liked *Alice's Adventures*, and I must say this is the first time he and I have had creative differences over a film. He seemed to be the only child in an otherwise noisy and listless audience who was paying any attention. He kept saying to his mother, "When is Alice going home?" And I kept saying to his mother, "When is John going home?"

Fiona Fullerton[66] as Alice was excellent; so were the sets and the special effects. But the thing that was really missing, that is present in all great stories and films for children, like *The Wizard of Oz*, was the element of danger. Alice is never fearful or apprehensive about the strange creatures or weird places she encounters.

Since the film was so dramatically ineffective, I kept wondering what was keeping my son quiet, aside from his three boxes of popcorn; then I realized that in his sophisticated way, as a fan of *Dragnet*, he must have spotted Alice as a teenage junkie. Whenever she felt too small, she popped some kind of unlabeled pill or liquid to make herself bigger. Whenever she felt too big, she popped something else to bring herself down. Nine times I counted her popping uppers and downers. She popped everything from Alice B. Toklas[67] cookies to psychedelic mushrooms. Who else but a junkie would crawl into a rabbit hole and call it Wonderland?

That's why nothing bothered her. When she falls into a bottomless pit, she isn't afraid. She just smiles and thinks she's on a cool trip to China. And who else but somebody on a high would enjoy talking to a four foot frog? (My son doesn't actually talk to his; he listens to it.)

My son said he wanted to see Alice again, and I can't imagine why... unless maybe it's for another popcorn fix.

So John liked the story I'd told him about when I took my three-year old daughter, Corrie, to see *Bambi*.

"Oh, yes," John said. "I think the readers will appreciate it."

"Well, it was a mommy and Corrie day, and *Bambi* was being brought back to theaters for a limited run and that's where we went one Saturday, leaving her older brother and younger sister home with their father. The theater was filled with parents with their small children. Corrie was seemingly enjoying the movie but then I became somewhat concerned with the forest fire scene and all those animals running in hopes of escaping. There was the frantic flames accompanied by background music that sounded like a screeching Nelson Eddy[68] and Jeanette Macdonald[69]. All around the theater parents were comforting their children, letting them know it was going to be okay when my daughter tugged on my sleeve. I leaned in, ready to calm her, but in a matter-of-fact whisper, she said, 'Mommy, I know why all those animals are running away.' I nodded since it was obvious, but she had a different explanation. 'To get away from that awful music.'

John, I knew I was going to have my hands full with that one as she grew up, but I'm happy to report that she is now a CPA and doing very well in her life."

"Yes, I love that story," John said. "Now we go from *Bambi* to *Deep Throat*."

"Wow, that is certainly a switch; however, I do believe there are a lot of so-called sex kittens called Bambi. So I guess *Deep Throat* was the other film you found difficult to review."

John went on to tell me that he was asked to review the porn flick after Jackie Kennedy[70] had been photographed leaving the theater. "I knew I could not review the content, so I did the same as I did with *Death Race 2000* and reviewed the experience," he said. "Only instead of taking my son, I took my wife. In my review, I described the long lines, the bowed heads, my wife not wanting to sign a legal release at the box office, people telling her to hurry as she took her time to read it, needing to squeeze past people to get to our seats, walking on a sticky floor. And then leaving. The closing line of the review was not permitted on air. Just in the magazine."

"Was it considered offensive?" I wanted to know.

"Only for broadcast," John said. "Not print. But that led me into court."

I didn't understand how that could be possible. After all, John was just reviewing the movie; he had no part in making it.

"A lawyer called me to be an expert witness," he explained. "He was defending a theater owner in Orange County arrested for showing the film. He offered me $300.00 or so to appear in what was a free speech trial. I declined the money but agreed to appear. The court was packed. It was a big media deal and covered by the news. After the attorney described my award-winning background on the *AM Show* and awards as KNBC's Critic-at-Large, he asked if I felt the owner was involved in a free speech issue. I said no. The filmmakers were and had the right to make it. But it is not free. Millions of us paid five bucks to see it, including the First Lady. If anything, we should all be arrested for encouraging such films. Carol, the audience howled."

"Audience, John? Wasn't this in a courtroom?"

John laughed and said, "Yes, but the spectators in the courtroom felt like an audience. Anyway, then the lawyer asked if I reviewed it. I said not the content, just the experience of taking my wife. He then asked if the broadcast review was the same. I said except for the last line, which only appeared in *LA Magazine*. He asked why I didn't broadcast it. I paused, and then said that I didn't talk that way in public. At that point I heard chuckles from those in the courtroom. The lawyer prodded, 'What was the last line, Mr. Barbour?' I said nothing until the judge told me that I could answer. I told him, 'Your honor, I do not like to talk like that in public and never did even in a nightclub.' He replied, 'Mr. Barbour, you're in a courtroom now. And no matter what you say, I assure you I've heard worse crap.'

"Very quietly I said, 'I wrote that my wife and I left after the first 15 inches.' Well, Carol, there was a volcanic eruption of howling and clapping. The building shook with laughter. The judge almost fell off his chair before he took his gavel and banged it, saying, 'Case dismissed.' When it was over, the judge told me he never saw a conviction ever in any case that ended in laughter."

"Well, John, I think maybe here is a good place to move ahead and away from *Deep Throat.*

A name that raises the hackles of other people over the years is Jane Fonda[71], and all because of the picture of her on a North Vietnamese anti-aircraft gun earning her the name, "Hanoi Jane." John writes about Jane in his memoir and how much he respected her but also his concerns when he had her on his talk show. It's an interesting story, to be sure.

As for me, I've always liked Jane Fonda. I have been watching the Netflix series, *Grace and Frankie*, starring her and Lily Tomlin, for the second time. And even though her part was small on *The Newsroom*, Jane's character of Leona Lansing felt authentic in every way.

That said, three years prior to *On Golden Pond*, the movie that Jane starred in with her father, Henry Fonda[72] and Katharine Hepburn[73], and went on to get ten Academy Award nominations and win three: Best Actor for Henry Fonda, Best Actress for Katharine Hepburn and Best Adapted Screenplay, was the movie *Comes a Horseman*. Here's John's review:

I walk out of a lot of movies. Sometimes people ask me if perhaps as a critic I don't owe it to the filmmakers to watch their work in its entirety. That might be true if I were walking in with the thought that I was there strictly to review the film, when in fact I walk into every film with the expectation that I'm going to enjoy it. I walk in feeling more like a member of the audience than a critic. And when I like a film I walk out at the end still feeling like part of the audience. It's the bummers that turn me into a critic. However, at the point in a movie where I feel the filmmakers and I have made a serious mistake, I am doing them and myself a disservice by staying. Prolonging the agony of a mediocre movie not only makes me angrier with myself but, what's worse, it makes me more hostile and impatient with the people causing it.

On the average, even if I know within five minutes that a film is going to be a dog, I give it at least half an hour to grab me—that's the length of a good TV sitcom. Only once have I made an exception to that half-hour rule, and that was with *Comes a Horseman*, starring Jane Fonda and James Caan[74]. I gave this an additional 10 minutes out of respect and admiration for Alan Pakula,[75] who is probably one of America's classiest, most tasteful and most underrated directors. Years after seeing *The Parallax View* I still savor the craftsmanship of that hauntingly effective film. Pakula's name on *Comes a Horseman* is what got me to go into the theater in the first place, while Irwin Winkler[76] and Robert Chartoff's[77] names as executive producers would normally have kept me out.

In order to capture a feeling of authenticity in *Barry Lyndon*, Stanley Kubrick[78] lit his interior scenes with candles. In *Horseman*, Pakula seems to have tried to go him one better by lighting his with matches. Either that or cameraman Gordon Willis[79] forgot to take the cover off his lens. Forty minutes should give you enough time to see if you're going to like any movie, but in order to form an opinion, you've first got to be *able* to see it. If it had been a TV movie I would have gotten up and turned the contrast knob. Or called a repairman.

The sound worked, though, which was also unfortunate, because what I could hear sounded terrible. The only thing duller than that lighting was the script. I got the impression Fonda owned a lot of farmland and Jason Robards[80] wanted it for his cattle and her for himself. Caan hires on as a helping hand after being shot in the stomach by a gunman hired by Robards. All of which sounds like a plot in every one of Republic Pictures' westerns. When Republic made these films, however, at least you could see them. Maybe that's why they went out of business.

As I read this review, I couldn't help but wonder if any of our younger readers would understand what John meant when he mentioned turning the contrast knob on a TV. I also realized that the biggest criticism that John had was to do with the lighting and nothing was said about the acting. Therefore, I did a Google search to check out some reviews and the response to *Come a Horseman* was lukewarm. However, since Jane Fonda stars in this, I may still want to take up a couple hours and watch it.

Notes

1 https://en.wikipedia.org/wiki/Harris_%26_Frank
2 https://en.wikipedia.org/wiki/Jack_Albertson
3 https://en.wikipedia.org/wiki/Sam_Levene
4 https://en.wikipedia.org/wiki/George_Burns
5 https://en.wikipedia.org/wiki/Walter_Matthau
6 https://en.wikipedia.org/wiki/Richard_Benjamin
7 https://en.wikipedia.org/wiki/Burt_Reynolds
8 https://en.wikipedia.org/wiki/Charlton_Heston
9 https://en.wikipedia.org/wiki/Chuck_Connors
10 https://en.wikipedia.org/wiki/Bryant_Gumbel
11 https://en.wikipedia.org/wiki/Eddie_Albert
12 https://en.wikipedia.org/wiki/Vince_Lombardi
13 Fictional character in the novel The Caine Mutiny (1951) by Herman Wouk.
14 https://en.wikipedia.org/wiki/Albert_S._Ruddy
15 https://en.wikipedia.org/wiki/Robert_Aldrich
16 https://en.wikipedia.org/wiki/Tracy_Keenan_Wynn
17 https://en.wikipedia.org/wiki/Jackie_Gleason
18 https://en.wikipedia.org/wiki/Jerry_Reed
19 https://en.wikipedia.org/wiki/Pat_McCormick_(actor)
20 https://en.wikipedia.org/wiki/Paul_Williams_(songwriter)
21 https://en.wikipedia.org/wiki/Eddie_Fisher_(singer)
22 https://en.wikipedia.org/wiki/Elizabeth_Taylor
23 https://en.wikipedia.org/wiki/Sally_Field
24 https://en.wikipedia.org/wiki/George_%22Gabby%22_Hayes
25 https://en.wikipedia.org/wiki/Virginia_Christine
26 https://en.wikipedia.org/wiki/Richard_Nixon
27 https://en.wikipedia.org/wiki/Mike_Douglas
28 https://en.wikipedia.org/wiki/Dinah_Shore
29 https://en.wikipedia.org/wiki/Jerry_Belson
30 https://en.wikipedia.org/wiki/Darren_McGavin
31 https://en.wikipedia.org/wiki/Ali_MacGraw
32 https://en.wikipedia.org/wiki/Dom_DeLuise
33 https://en.wikipedia.org/wiki/Sid_Caesar
34 https://en.wikipedia.org/wiki/Alfred_Hitchcock
35 https://en.wikipedia.org/wiki/James_Stewart
36 https://en.wikipedia.org/wiki/Jim_Garrison

37 https://en.wikipedia.org/wiki/Sam_Peckinpah
38 https://en.wikipedia.org/wiki/Hugh_Hefner
39 https://en.wikipedia.org/wiki/Steve_McQueen
40 https://en.wikipedia.org/wiki/James_Cagney
41 https://en.wikipedia.org/wiki/Humphrey_Bogart
42 https://en.wikipedia.org/wiki/Edward_G._Robinson
43 https://en.wikipedia.org/wiki/Sally_Struthers
44 https://en.wikipedia.org/wiki/Shelley_Winters
45 https://en.wikipedia.org/wiki/Brian_Keith
46 https://en.wikipedia.org/wiki/Jerry_Lewis
47 https://en.wikipedia.org/wiki/The_Jerry_Lewis_MDA_Labor_Day_Telethon
48 https://en.wikipedia.org/wiki/Jack_Nicholson
49 https://en.wikipedia.org/wiki/Alan_Ladd
50 https://en.wikipedia.org/wiki/Toby_Stephens
51 https://en.wikipedia.org/wiki/Paul_Rudd
52 https://en.wikipedia.org/wiki/Mira_Sorvino
53 https://en.wikipedia.org/wiki/Leonardo_DiCaprio
54 https://en.wikipedia.org/wiki/Tobey_Maguire
55 https://en.wikipedia.org/wiki/Baz_Luhrmann
56 https://en.wikipedia.org/wiki/Barry_Diller
57 https://en.wikipedia.org/wiki/Robert_Evans
58 https://en.wikipedia.org/wiki/Robert_Redford
59 https://en.wikipedia.org/wiki/Laurence_Olivier
60 https://en.wikipedia.org/wiki/Mia_Farrow
61 https://en.wikipedia.org/wiki/Jack_Clayton
62 https://en.wikipedia.org/wiki/Real_People
63 https://en.wikipedia.org/wiki/Greg_Kinnear
64 https://en.wikipedia.org/wiki/Tom_Jones_(singer)
65 https://en.wikipedia.org/wiki/Doris_Day
66 https://en.wikipedia.org/wiki/Fiona_Fullerton
67 https://en.wikipedia.org/wiki/Alice_B._Toklas
68 https://en.wikipedia.org/wiki/Nelson_Eddy
69 https://en.wikipedia.org/wiki/Jeanette_MacDonald
70 https://en.wikipedia.org/wiki/Jacqueline_Kennedy_Onassis
71 https://en.wikipedia.org/wiki/Jane_Fonda
72 https://en.wikipedia.org/wiki/Henry_Fonda
73 https://en.wikipedia.org/wiki/Katharine_Hepburn

74 https://en.wikipedia.org/wiki/James_Caan
75 https://en.wikipedia.org/wiki/Alan_J._Pakula
76 https://en.wikipedia.org/wiki/Irwin_Winkler
77 https://en.wikipedia.org/wiki/Robert_Chartoff
78 https://en.wikipedia.org/wiki/Stanley_Kubrick
79 https://en.wikipedia.org/wiki/Gordon_Willis
80 https://en.wikipedia.org/wiki/Jason_Robards

III. John of All Trades

In getting to know John, I realized that we are similar in that we were forced to be "Jacks of all Trades." For me, I'm a writer, publicist, editor, blogger and consultant. I did it all because I had to survive once I was divorced and depended on myself. As for John, he did standup comedy, hosted a talk show, created a hit TV show and made award-winning documentaries. Like me, John felt lucky to be able to do so well while being a Jack of all trades, but when it came to being asked to be film critic, he said, "So I had wanted to know who would take such a multi-tasker seriously as a critic?" John hesitated, looked to be thinking, before he added, "Outside of LA, I was unknown or even ignored as a film critic. What I couldn't figure out is that *The LA Times* hired the previous critic whom I'd already mentioned, Burt Prelutsky, at *LA Magazine* to write a column. And here I was on TV, 20 times better known and more widely read than Burt. I would have loved to done a general column for the *Times*, to write about the War, Civil Rights, life. But the call never came." Then with a twinkle in his eye, he added, "Maybe it was because I bombed their heralded film critic Charles Champlin[1]. I'd said that he never met a movie or starlet he didn't like. This led to a cursing, screaming call from his wife."

"John, it's as if you invite trouble."

"No, Carol. Trouble just shows up when you tell the truth. But let me ask you a question."

"Okay."

"Why are you writing a book about me and my reviews? Why not Pauline Kael[2], Frank Rich[3], Gene Shalit[4], or Siskel[5] & Ebert[6]?"

"Well, the easy answer is that I didn't know them personally, but in reality, after working with you on your memoir and knowing just how interesting of a life you've had and are still having, I think people need to get to know who you are and all that you've accomplished. Your life could have taken such a different, even tragic, path so I think the aforementioned critics already had their recognition, so to speak, and it's about time you got yours. Which brings us back to more movie reviews."

Doing this book with John sometimes informs me of movies that I'd missed for one reason or another and wish I hadn't. One in particular is *The Sugarland Express* starring Goldie Hawn[7] and William Atherton[8], but more importantly directed by Steven Spielberg[9], which was his debut. Here's John's review:

Some of the best moments in the cop movies are the chase scenes, so it was only a matter of time before someone finally said, "Wouldn't it be terrific if we just filmed one big chase scene?"

That someone evidently was director Steven Spielberg and the movie is *The Sugarland Express*. He was right; it is terrific.

Goldie Hawn plays a young mother who has been declared unfit by the Texas Welfare Dept., which takes her child and places him with permanent foster parents in a little town called Sugarland. So when Goldie gets out of prison, she coerces her husband into leaving a prison farm earlier than the law would want him to in order to help retrieve her son.

They hitch a ride with an old couple whose smokemobile is stopped by a state trooper for going 25 mph on the expressway. While the trooper is writing out a ticket, the couple steal the car, then when the trooper stops them for going 85 mph where there is no expressway, they steal his car and him. Then the Sugarland Expressway starts, hundreds of cop cars and a TV newsman trailing the hi-jacked cop car looking for an opportunity to capture them, kill them, or interview them.

Goldie will only stop at stations that give trading stamps, and at one point, with no restrooms around, the whole caravan stops while they temporarily hijack a truck with an outhouse on it. There are many humorous moments in the film, but the film is not primarily funny; it is primarily real, and underlying some of the fine tragi-comic moments is an ever-present horror of what is going to happen to this couple, a horror that grows the more we get to know them.

Everything about *Sugarland* is excellent, from a perfect script written by Hal Barwood[10] and Matthew Robbins[11] to the outstanding performances. But I would say the star of *Sugarland Express* is director Spielberg, who has made a debut with a distinctively American movie. His career should itself become a Sugarland express.

I would have to say that John was right about Spielberg. A 1975 major summer hit, *Jaws,* was directed by our wunderkind. I'd read the novel by Peter Benchley[12] prior to seeing the movie and later read that Benchley regretted having written the book, believing that it encouraged "excessive fear and unnecessary culls of such an important predator in ocean ecosystems and became an advocate for marine conservation." Either way, theaters were filled with screaming patrons as the shark went about terrorizing a beach community called Amity Island. So what did John think about this movie?

There's a real film-feast this summer, but *Jaws* is still the only one you can sink your teeth into

by John Barbour

Because of the immense amount of film it grinds out for TV and theaters, Universal is sometimes known as the sausage factory of cinema. However with *Jaws*, they have finally turned out a prime rib…or at least a fillet. At times *Jaws* is so good it doesn't even look like a Universal film. The script trims away some excess character fat from the book and gets right to the heart of the matter—and right to yours.

In disaster films like *Earthquake* and *Towering Inferno*, nothing ever happens to kids and dogs. In *Jaws* they are the second course on the menu. Because of that and the sight of a few dismembered limbs, be cautious about letting your children see it.

For the first hour, director Steven Spielberg does not let us so much as glimpse the giant killer shark, just its leftovers, creating terror and tension which make the first half of the film an *Exorcist* with fins. Spielberg uses the audience's fear of the unseen to its fullest. In an attempt to catch the shark, an old man puts a pot roast on a big hook and ties the rope to the end of the pier. We just see the rope being pulled away along with the end of the pier and the old man. Then we see the pier stop and start "swimming" back.

There are also some frighteningly funny moments. Richard Dreyfuss[13], as the shark expert, cuts open one shark to prove to Roy Scheider[14], the resort island's police chief, it's not the White Killer—that this one just came up from warm water. In support of his claim, he pulls a Louisiana license plate out of its stomach.

The second half is an excellent adventure film with Robert Shaw[15], possessed like a modern Captain Ahab, going from Moby Mean with a vengeance. The actors are perfect, and Bob Mattey's[16] special effects are superb. His mechanical shark not only takes people out of the water but boards boats to get food to go. It's not the kind of thing you forget in a hurry. After seeing *Jaws*, a lot of people are going to be afraid to go in the shallow end of the shower.

Apparently, Spielberg had impressed John, and the director went on to make some more brilliant movies, including *Close Encounters of the Third Kind, Star Wars, Raiders of the Lost Ark* and one of my all-time favorites, *E.T. the Extra-Terrestrial*, but I asked John's feelings on *Schindler's List*, which admittedly, I cannot bring myself to watch; the world is tragic enough without my being "entertained" by such historical horror.

John said, "I enjoyed many of his [Spielberg] movies, but this is weird, I always had the feeling a slick craftsman was at the helm, someone who could entertain me, but one who never involved or inspired me."

I wasn't sure I knew what John meant, so I pressed him further.

"To me," he said, "Spielberg first never told the total story of Schindler[17], and his movie often seemed like a documentary on how to murder Jews. Six million of them. Numbers so vast we cannot comprehend, or worse, feel it. So, this brings me to not favorite films but the best films in their category. And the best film ever made about the indescribable horror of the Nazi genocide of Jews was a 1965 Czech film called *The Shop on Main Street*. There's only one Jew in it, the sweet elderly lady shop owner. We can identify with one. Not six million. When the Germans take over, they order that her mentally challenged Aryan janitor now should run the place. What happens to these once dear friends at the end is so devastatingly heartbreaking, my wife and I had to sit for ten teary minutes before we could get up. That is what art can do; rare in movies."

I had to agree and was reminded of when I brought my young daughters to see *My Girl*. It looked to be a charming, sweet movie and I thought it would be a fun day out. I had no idea of what would happen to a very young Macaulay Culkin's[18] character in this coming-of-age story, but once the credits were rolling, Natasha, my youngest was sobbing on my shoulder, asking me in no uncertain terms why I would bring her to such a movie. Talk about heartbreaking.

But I have to say that I am a lot like Natasha when it comes to certain movies. I appreciate certain flicks for the quality of the work while asking myself why I would put myself emotionally through the ordeal of watching it. This happened to me when my then husband got me to agree to go see *The Deer Hunter* with him while we were on an anniversary get-away in Lake Placid. I'm not a fan of war movies and certainly didn't think it would make me feel very "warm and fuzzy" but he had wanted to see it for quite some time, so I agreed. I sat next to him in the theater for about the first twenty minutes or so until the scene where naked Vietnamese children were running from gunfire. I immediately got up and ran out of that theater sobbing, refusing to go back in. I had no desire to see children gunned down. So we went back to the hotel that night, both of us in a less-than accommodating mood. But the story doesn't end there.

A week or so later, back home, friends of ours, a couple, wanted us to go to the movies with them and they really wanted to see the movie that was garnering a lot of positive attention. Yes, *The Deer Hunter.* I agreed to go, saying now that I knew what to expect, I'd be able to handle it better. Curiously enough, once that scene came up, those children being chased by gunfire, my friends leaned over and whispered something to me that I wasn't able to make out, but they stood up and walked out of the theater. I turned to my husband saying that they, too, were upset by that scene, or I assumed as much, so we got up and went into the lobby. They weren't anywhere to be found until moments later, the husband came out of the men's restroom and his wife came out of the women's restroom. They gave my then husband and me an odd look as they started back into the theater.

I said, "Wait, I thought you wanted to leave."

The wife said, "Leave? Why?"

"Because…because…those poor children."

The couple laughed and said that they only happened to have to use the bathroom at the same time, but were eager to get into the theater. So there we were, the four of us skulking back into the darkened theater looking for our seats with me disappointed that I'd have to sit through a war movie, albeit a very well made one.

"Well, that movie had an impressive cast," John said.

That I had to agree to. With Meryl Streep[19], Robert De Niro[20], Christopher Walken[21] and many others, that was a movie one couldn't forget, as much as I tried.

Switching gears, sort of, John wanted to know what I thought of *The Godfather*, which came out in 1972. I told him that I don't remember who I saw it with, when or even what theater, but what I do remember in spite of all the violence and murder on humans, is that horse's head, which upset me more than anything else.

"Well, Carol," John said, "As far as I'm concerned, it's the best gangster movie ever made. It's so good that it has you cheering for the mafia."

If you're wondering what John thought of the follow up, *Godfather Part II*, which came out in 1974, I'll let him tell you himself:

Godfather II: Two!...Two!...Two!

By John Barbour

On second viewing, the second generation is still only second rate.

Godfather II is the only movie I've ever gone back to see a second time after not liking it the first time—I went to see if I would feel the same about it after all the rave reviews, especially Pauline Kael's in *The New Yorker*. But after trying unsuccessfully to sit through it a second time, what I ended up feeling different about was Pauline Kael; she must have watched it with her eyes still smudged with butter from *Last Tango*. Kael is a brilliant writer, but when it comes to writing critically about foreign directors, Robert Altman[22], Marlon Brando[23]—and Francis Ford Coppola[24]—she sounds like a woman who has gone through a premature *mentalpause*.

After bombing the film on the six o'clock news, I received an angry letter from Paramount Pictures—one of three studios which had previously barred me from their lot. In it, account executive Hank Ehrlich[25] claimed that I had given an irresponsible review of a film that had cost a great deal of money to make, and one which everyone else loved. My response to Ehrlich was a Xeroxed letter that I have been pulling out of the file for over a year now and sending to anyone whose arguments for liking something were its cost and the fact that everybody else liked it. That Xeroxed letter reads: "THE COMMITTEE TO REELECT THE PRESIDENT SPENT MORE MONEY, AND NIXON WON EVERY STATE BUT MASSACHUSETTS. THANKS FOR TAKING THE TROUBLE TO WRITE. WARMEST REGARDS, MASSACHUSETTS!"

When I went back to see the film, I went with somebody who had been involved with the project and who had an immense amount of faith in Coppola and the script's potential. But less than halfway through, my friend was slouched down in the seat moaning with anguished boredom and disappointment, commenting aloud that we were learning more about Italian holidays, funerals, weddings, christenings and marches than we were about the characters.

For me it was like going to a Frank Sinatra concert only to end up listening to Frank Sinatra Jr.[26] instead. The look is similar; the sound is similar; but there is no soul. You know if the father hadn't been so outstanding the son-of would have ended up waiting tables at Two Guys from Italy. The original *Godfather* was unquestionably a brilliantly crafted film. In *Godfather II* there were only two things that held my interest at all: the design and texture of the film itself, like the original, gave me the impression I was looking at authentic faded photographs; and Robert De Niro's performance as the young Vito Corleone was outstanding, if only because it brought Brando's presence back into the film.

The other performances—including Al Pacino's[27]—are too studiously low key and, like the film, lack a sense of urgency and pace. And that also means Lee Strasberg[28], the Method Messiah. Strasberg plays Hyman Roth, supposedly the most influential Jewish mobster in America. But with the exception of a single scene in which he asserts himself about the death of Moe Greene, who built Las Vegas, Strasberg plays Roth as though he were no more than a henpecked waiter at Art's Delicatessen.

Coppola's intercutting within certain scenes becomes tediously predictable. Whenever somebody is going to be killed he cuts back to a festival scene to point up the obvious contrast; thus, every time you see a festival you know there is going to be a killing, and every time there is a killing you know there is going to be a festival.

As for the plotting, it's like looking into a pot of spaghetti and trying to find both ends of the same strand. In *Godfather*, the characters created the events through which they moved; in *Godfather II* the filmmakers have created the events and tried to fit the characters into them. This makes the movie sometimes visual, but never visceral. Paramount gave Coppola artistic control over the film, if that's what you call it, but evidently he didn't exercise much critical control over himself.

After reading that review, it crossed my mind that maybe John's expectations were too high for something that would be a challenge to improve upon. But it did lead me to ask John about some other "best" movies.

"The best religious picture ever made," John said, "was *He Who Must Die*, which was directed by Jules Dassin[29], who had been blacklisted. It was a 1957 French film. The story was based on Nikos Kazantzakis's[30] novel, *Christ Recrucified*.

"Best heist film. There are a few but Stanley Kubrick's second film *The Killing* is my favorite. It was made in 1956 and based on the novel *Clean Break* by Lionel White[31]."

I interjected, "You told us about *Deep Throat* but I'd be curious to know what you think is the best erotic movie ever made."

"That's easy," John replied. "Italy's *Malizia* with Laura Antonelli[32], the most beautiful woman ever on film. She plays a frump housekeeper for a widower with three sons. The sixteen year-old son falls in love with her. His desire to just touch her stockinged ankle in a movie with no nudity is visual Viagra. But this brings me to a filmmaker I rank as the best ever, even over Kubrick, little known except to real film buffs and the French."

"Who?"

"Claude LeLouch[33], famous for *A Man and A Woman*. He made one of the best love stories ever. The couple doesn't meet till the end of the film at a New York airport. When they retrieve their luggage, his is on top of hers. Totally brilliant. He made over 30 films, credited in 60. He also made one of the greatest antiwar films outside of Kubrick's *Paths of Glory* and Trumbo's *Johnny Get your Gun*. I can't recall the French name but the premise is two successful bank robbers find their careers curtailed when the more efficient Germans take over France and the banks. And not a shot is fired."

"Without a doubt, John, you know your movies."

"But I'd be remiss if I didn't mention two more of the best antiwar films. Of course, they weren't made in America. The first is 1969's *Z* directed by Costa-Gravis[34]. And then there is the one of a kind, *The Battle of Algiers*, directed by Gillo Pontecorvo[35]. To this day it's screened annually by the CIA!"

Okay, so John told us his favorite movies, but I nudged him to tell us who he thought was America's best filmmaker.

He said, "Thanks for bringing me back. I can get carried away."

"You're enthusiastic and there's nothing wrong with that, John."

"Well your question for me is a no brainer. Stanley Kubrick. From one of his first films, *The Killing* with Sterling Hayden[36]. I already said it was the best heist film and then *Paths of Glory, The Shining, 2001: A Space Odyssey, Spartacus* where he and Kirk Douglas[37] ended blacklisting by hiring Dalton Trumbo to write it, to *Dr. Strangelove*, one of the greatest films ever made, and genius performances from Sterling Hayden and Peter Sellers[38]. Kubrick displays a visual vibrant intelligence that is totally unique. You can almost tell a Kubrick film by just the lighting and framing. He is missed."

Yet, as much as John appreciates a talent, if he feels that they have fallen short, he doesn't pretend to ignore it. No, he faces it head on and shares it with his readers, as he did for his review from February 1976, *Biting the Bullets & Bombs Through a Dog Day Year*, where he wrote about "1975 and some of its events."

This time, even Stanley Kubrick had trouble walking tall.

Beginning with *The Killing*, still one of the best caper films ever made, and continuing with films like *Paths of Glory, Dr. Strangelove* and *2001*, the *Citizen Kane* of science fiction, Stanley Kubrick has proved he is one of the few authentic masters of the medium. He has almost put as many stirring images on celluloid as Michelangelo[39] put on a ceiling; he is to the camera what Rubinstein[40] is to the piano.

That's why it's so sad to say that with his latest, *Barry Lyndon*, Kubrick kept doing it till he got it wrong. Watching it is like watching Hank Aaron[41] strike out or George Blanda[42] miss a field goal—you know there's greatness there, but it doesn't show.

The film is based on the William Thackeray[43] novel about a young 18th century Irishman who leaves home after fighting a duel over his cousin; he then joins the British and Prussian armies, becomes a gambler, marries wealth, then ends up alone. Kubrick, however, is so preoccupied with recreating the pace and the costumes of the period—rather than the characters—the film ends up looking and feeling like a *Great Gatsby* with 18th century wigs. Kubrick could have compensated for some of the lack of substance in the characters if he had hired an actor whose abilities and presence had at least a sense of mystery about them. But the makeup and costumes worn by Ryan O'Neal[44] as Barry Lyndon have more depth than his performance.

Another thing: in all his other movies, Kubrick has shown he is a master at selecting music. In *Strangelove*, he was the first to use nostalgic music; and *Also Spach Zarathustra*[45] is better known now as *The Theme from 2001*. But in *Barry Lyndon,* the director seems to have gone tone deaf. By underscoring the slowness of the scenes with even slower authentic 18th-century music, the film begins to sound like three and a half hours of maddening minuets. The movie was based on a 150 year-old book and the movie seemed to move at that pace. I felt like I was being dragged through an art gallery. To be sure, Kubrick's images are pretty; but you can get that on a calendar. And on a calendar you only have to look at it for a month.

I'm sure that was a difficult review to write about someone who John had admired for years. On the other side, I then asked John if there were some films he'd go see because of who had directed them.

"Absolutely, dozens. Because I felt they chose good material to begin with. An early one was Marty Scorsese[46]. I was invited to see his *Taxi Driver* at a Warner's screening by his friend and mine, Freddy Weintraub[47]. Freddy discovered Bruce Lee[48] for *Enter the Dragon* and owned The Bitter End night club in New York when I was doing standup comedy. A couple of years after seeing *Taxi Driver*, I heard he'd made a film Doris Day turned down called *Alice Doesn't Live Here Anymore* that Warners hated and was dumping, screening it only at one theater in Westwood. That's when I was doing reviews on Monday, Wednesday and Friday at KNBC. After Wednesday's news, I went by myself to see it. I loved it. The opening looked like a brief homage to *The Wizard of Oz*. Friday I reviewed it and said it was the perfect woman's picture and I was taking my wife Saturday to see it. The theater was packed. Monday Marty called me and asked if I'd call the brass at Warners who wanted to cut the opening clip. I did. The film was a huge hit. Months later the Calendar Section of *The LA Times* did a whole page on Marty, and Marty pointed out that I had saved his film from obscurity."

Here's John's review of *Alice Doesn't Live Here Anymore,* which can be caught occasionally on Turner Classic Movies:

There are some films that are called women's films because there is perhaps some aspect of the character or story that reflects an experience or an emotion that is uniquely feminine. While these films may involve the psyche of the female audience, I would say that as art they are half-successful (or half-failures) because they deny the male a real understanding of that experience, leaving him as an uninvolved spectator. That's why *Alice Doesn't Live Here Any More* with Ellen Burstyn[49] is to me one of the best movies about a woman that I've ever seen. It's done with such artistry, honesty and wit that it would even appeal to machos like Norman Mailer[50].

Burstyn plays a woman who, as a girl, wanted to end up like Alice Faye[51] in Hollywood. Instead, she ends up a 35-year-old widow in Socorro, New Mexico, whose marriage was such that she was more alone when her husband was alive. So she takes her 11-year-old son on the road back to Monterey—where she thinks she used to be happy—with $1.85 left after the funeral.

In Albuquerque, she gets a job in a dumpy bar singing in a voice she admits ain't no Peggy Lee[52], and after a chilling encounter with a younger married man, she and her child are forced to move on to Tucson where she works as a waitress and meets a divorced rancher, Kris Kristofferson[53]. The plot accordingly thickens.

You'll so love Burstyn and the humanity and humor in this inspired film that when it's over you'll want to sit in the theatre and enjoy the afterglow. In fact, at Academy Award time, when director Martin Scorsese and author Robert Getchell[54] may well be handed Oscars, no one will have to hand one to Ellen Burstyn. Oscar will run over and hug her.

As it happens, John was right: At the 47th Academy Awards, Burstyn won Best Actress.

John's opinion obviously mattered to directors since they often wanted him to preview their films. "It happened often," he said. "But I turned them all down, except for Robert Evans[55], Production Head at paramount."

John does tell the story in delicious detail in *Your Mother's Not a Virgin*, but I will share it briefly here.

"Evans wanted me to see *Black Sunday* privately, so I agreed. In it there's a scene in which Robert Shaw's character is trying to stop a terrorist from bombing The Super Bowl. Shaw is in the crowded stands. The terrorist is by the broadcast truck. Shaw has to warn them and starts leaping over fans. I pointed out to Evans that Shaw had a phone in his pocket. Evans should either add a short scene where the phone doesn't work…or trim it. He screamed, 'Fuck no! I spent 50 grand to shoot it!' He never added the line or trimmed it and the movie was the only bomb. We never talked again."

"Well, I'll still talk to you, John, even though you pointed out something in the *Wizard of Oz,* a movie I'd mentioned earlier that meant a lot to me, that I'd never considered before."

"I may be the only critic that pointed out that film's flaw, which is that the story is never resolved. The film opens with Margaret Hamilton[56] playing Miss Gulch, who was coming to take Toto to the pound. She, of course, later appears as the wonderfully played Wicked Witch. And all the characters we see in the opening also appear in Dorothy's dream. When the dream is over and she wakes up, and exclaims, 'There's no place like home'…even in Kansas, where the threat to Toto still exists!"

I believe John makes a valid point, but I'm going to believe that Miss Gulch somehow gave up her quest to take Dorothy's precious pup away. But that was a film made before John was reviewing movies. And then there was the movie he said that was one of the worst, most disappointing movies he ever saw long after he stopped being a critic—at least professionally.

"Unfortunately, because it was not only the worst film I ever saw, but the most repugnantly dishonest to history and deserved to be widely trashed. I was so appalled at it that I did a YouTube review of it a few years ago, which got thousands of hits."

"So you did review it!" I said, prodding John to tell me the name of this debacle.

"Oh, I'm sorry. I so loathed it, I don't even want to mention it. *Once Upon a Time in Hollywood*. I loved Quentin Tarantino's[57] *Pulp Fiction*. Quentin can write great dialogue. Since I lived in LA at the time of the brutal bloody Sharon Tate[58] murders, I was anxious to see how he would handle them because there were serious doubts about those murders. Potheads do not climb telephone poles to cut wires. Not only did Quentin not touch on them, he erased from history the horrible truths of what happened to the victims and America, but instead had one of the stars kill the killers, giving the impression the corpses lived happily ever after. I will never look at another film of his again, even if paid to do so."

As it happens, my daughter, Natasha, and her boyfriend had been looking forward to seeing this movie. I suppose it helped that Leonardo DiCaprio and Brad Pitt[59] were in it and gave it some cachet. They were vaguely aware of the Manson[60] murders, but didn't really grasp just how tragic it was. Regrettably, they saw the movie before seeing John's review because my daughter said it was two hours and 40 minutes of her life that she'd never get back and that, after both she and her boyfriend watched John's review of it, said it was spot on.

I then asked John if there were other director-writers' films that he felt the same way about as he did Tarantino.

"Carol, I'm so glad you said director-writers because they are the real filmmakers. More than just directors. So here is where I must mention Woody Allen[61]."

Before we talk about Woody Allen, how about I share your reviews for some of his movies, starting with a brief write up *for Play It Again, Sam* (1972). You wrote, *Woody Allen's irresistible adaptation of his own Broadway hit comedy about a Mitty-like film critic who is queer for Bogey movies and enlists his hero's help in making it in the world, especially with dames. There isn't a schtick in the film you haven't seen before, but you laugh in spite of yourself.*

Now here's your review of *The Front* (1976) starring Zero Mostel[62] and Woody.

The Front: Soft on Blacklisting

By John Barbour

For those who think that blacklisting of some Americans in the '50s for their political associations was no more inconveniencing than getting a parking ticket, and for those who like their social commentary in films fluffy and soft, with no more substance than a donut, than *The Front* starring Woody Allen, which is supposed to be about blacklisting, is very pleasantly digestible. For those, however, who feel otherwise, who would like to see a real meaty movie about that era, *The Front's* filmmakers who were themselves blacklisted offer nothing to chew on but the hole. The hole is that *The Front* could have used any other premise; it looks into blacklisting with about as much conviction as some Teamsters looking into the disappearance of Jimmy Hoffa.[63] The film opens with a 1953 newsreel composite which includes footage of Joe McCarthy's[64] wedding, the Rosenbergs[65], and the Korean War, with Sinatra's voice-over singing "Young at Heart." It's an excellent bittersweet sequence. It leads us to expect a story with a sharp, satiric edge and a ring of reality…

which never happens.

In probably his best performance, Woody Allen plays a small-time bookmaker in the early '50s who thinks the Red Menace is the team that beats the Dodgers. As a favor to a friend who has been blacklisted as a TV writer, Woody begins to front for him at ten percent. Soon he so loves the sweet smell of success and the liberal associate producer (Andrea Marcovicci[66]) so much he takes on two more clients. Zero Mostel badly overplays a suddenly blacklisted TV superstar who, in order to get clearance to work, is forced to spy on Woody. But the tragedy in the film here is that there is no sense of tragedy. There are some funny moments, though; especially when Woody takes it on himself to tell one of this writers why the guy's script doesn't work. But *The Front* lacks the urgency, truth, and irony of the opening, primarily because Director Marty Ritt[67] and writer Walter Bernstein[68] seem afraid themselves to name names or face facts.

If they are reluctant to speak up, they could have gone back to showing actual newscasts with some of the real personalities involved. To some—the donut lovers--this mild, amusing movie may be hard to resist. For others, the fact it's so soft on blacklisting may make it hard to take.

Woody Allen Is Annie Hall

By John Barbour

Woody Allen's *Annie Hall* shouldn't have been called *Annie Hall*; it should have been called *Woody Allen*. It seems that this time out Allen didn't have anything else to write about, so he decided to write about himself: a nebbish New York writer-comedian whose enormous public success is built on his supposedly enormous private failings; a sometimes endearingly compulsive misfit who spends all his time waiting for psychiatrists, sex and laughs. And talk about waiting for laughs—in Annie Hall, while you don't have to wait long for the first one, it feels as though you have to wait forever for the second.

The film opens with Allen looking directly into the camera and talking about how much more attractive and virile he will become now that he's reached 40. He then goes on to wonder out loud about the demise of his relationship with Annie (Diane Keaton)[69], a struggling actress who is trying to be a struggling singer. The two meet on a New York tennis court and part in a Hollywood health-food restaurant and, in between, we watch them trying to make small talk, trying to make love, trying to make up, trying to make house, and trying to make lobster thermidor. And watching them do all this is—in a word—trying.

Allen is a sometimes-brilliant gag writer, but he appears about as interested in real character development and film discipline as the Pope is in bar mitzvahs. Even when being autobiographical, a disciplined craftsman can be self-revealing, but all Allen reveals in this film is a glib self-indulgence that turns him into a Jewish John Cassavetes[70]. The charming idiosyncrasies in Keaton's character are not provided by the writer but by the performer, because Allen doesn't write people, he only writes straight men. In *Annie Hall*, when he runs out of straight men, he just drops in brief film clips of himself doing a college concert or being interviewed on the *Dick Cavett*[71] *Show*.

As in all Woody Allen films, there are some great on-line gags—and, as usual, some are so inside that nobody outside Manhattan or Bel-Air will understand them. But by displaying the kind of and-then-I wrote self-aggrandizement in *Annie Hall* that would've given even Ted Baxter[72] pause. Allen will bore some who ordinarily like Woody Allen films.

First, since this had been written several decades ago, I feel I must explain to our younger readers that John Cassavetes was a successful American actor, director and screenwriter while Ted Baxter flawlessly played a vain and shallow character on *The Mary Tyler Moore Show*.[73] But what stands out to me in John's review, especially now knowing what kind of being Woody Allen is, is how he points out the way Woody looks "directly into the camera and talking about how much more attractive and virile he will become now that he's reached 40." The very idea of this is unsettling.

John says, "As a writer-director, Woody has been a consummate American, mostly New Yorker, filmmaker. He's made a number of highly entertaining and interesting personal people films and his *Match Point* (2005) about a guy who happily gets away with murder tops anything Hitchcock did, including *Psycho*. But, evidently, according to an HBO documentary, *Allen v. Farrow*, and a statement from an Attorney General, he has gotten away with criminal pedophilia."

I admit that I haven't seen the whole documentary, but what I did see was, well, the word "unsettling" crops up again.

"As an actor," John continues, "I found him unappealing to look at but funny to listen to, which I thought was probably the only way he could get girls but I found out otherwise. See, in the late '60's, my act followed his at Mister Kelly's, a Chicago nightclub, as Dionne Warwick's[74] opening act. Jeff Wald[75], who was owner George Marienthal's[76] assistant, would come into my dressing room to keep me and Sarita company. After the third night, I asked Jeff why he was there. He said that his boss told him he had to keep every comic company because they were so insecure. He listed a bunch of comedians, but said Woody was the worst. Every night Jeff was ordered to go find him a girl. I told Jeff I had my girl and that he could leave. Like Tarrantino's films, I could not watch another of Woody's films, new or old."

I understood John's feelings, although I still listen to Michael Jackson's[77] music even after the accusations. But I have to admit that I was never a huge Woody Allen fan. I just found him to be a self-absorbed complainer. However, I asked John if he let something personal about someone influence his judgment of their work as artists and if it ever crept into a review.

"I'm only human, and do not like people who act inhumanly," John replied. "Or stupid. Oops. I should not have said 'stupid' because that is very human. And I've done that, too. Carol, when I was a struggling comic, I loved Mort Sahl[78], who was JFK's favorite comic. But he was the most vindictive, angry human I ever met. Yet, it never affected my appreciation of his comic genius."

After knowing John for a number of years now, one thing I am certain is that he doesn't usually censor himself, but working with him on his memoir I know that sometimes saying what he believes has given him some challenges, especially when speaking of politics.

"That's right," John says. "When I was hosting the AM Show, I had on Republican Governor Reagan[79] who was running for re-election, so I also had to have a Democrat and then a Socialist."

"I believe that was because of the Fairness Doctrine," I said.

"That and Equal time provisions. It was so strong that in 1968 when NBC sent Producer Walter Sheridan[80] to New Orleans with orders to destroy Jim Garrison's upcoming trial against Clay Shaw[81] for conspiracy to kill Kennedy and was recorded bribing Perry Russo[82], a key witness, the FCC ordered NBC to give Garrison equal time. After, Garrison went on late night blaming the CIA and not Oswald[83]. When Reagan became president, The Fairness Doctrine was abolished. That's when our news went from news to opinion, especially at Fox."

That led me to ask if critics wanted equal time in response to John's severely critical reviews.

"Sure, but it was usually the producers. But management always said no. It was forgotten, except once, and that was for *Soylent Green*, which we already discussed.

He was right so I figured it was time to move on.

Notes

1 https://en.wikipedia.org/wiki/Charles_Champlin
2 https://en.wikipedia.org/wiki/Pauline_Kael
3 https://en.wikipedia.org/wiki/Frank_Rich
4 https://en.wikipedia.org/wiki/Gene_Shalit
5 https://en.wikipedia.org/wiki/Gene_Siskel
6 https://en.wikipedia.org/wiki/Roger_Ebert
7 https://en.wikipedia.org/wiki/Goldie_Hawn
8 https://en.wikipedia.org/wiki/William_Atherton
9 https://en.wikipedia.org/wiki/Steven_Spielberg
10 https://en.wikipedia.org/wiki/Hal_Barwood
11 https://en.wikipedia.org/wiki/Matthew_Robbins_(screenwriter)
12 https://en.wikipedia.org/wiki/Peter_Benchley
13 https://en.wikipedia.org/wiki/Richard_Dreyfuss
14 https://en.wikipedia.org/wiki/Roy_Scheider
15 https://en.wikipedia.org/wiki/Robert_Shaw_(actor)
16 https://en.wikipedia.org/wiki/Robert_A._Mattey
17 https://en.wikipedia.org/wiki/Oskar_Schindler
18 https://en.wikipedia.org/wiki/Macaulay_Culkin
19 https://en.wikipedia.org/wiki/Meryl_Streep
20 https://en.wikipedia.org/wiki/Robert_De_Niro
21 https://en.wikipedia.org/wiki/Christopher_Walken
22 https://en.wikipedia.org/wiki/Robert_Altman
23 https://en.wikipedia.org/wiki/Marlon_Brando
24 https://en.wikipedia.org/wiki/Francis_Ford_Coppola
25 https://www.spoke.com/people/henry-ehrlich-3e1429c09e597c100146c145
26 https://en.wikipedia.org/wiki/Frank_Sinatra_Jr.
27 https://en.wikipedia.org/wiki/Al_Pacino
28 https://en.wikipedia.org/wiki/Lee_Strasberg
29 https://en.wikipedia.org/wiki/Jules_Dassin
30 https://en.wikipedia.org/wiki/Nikos_Kazantzakis
31 https://en.wikipedia.org/wiki/Lionel_White
32 https://en.wikipedia.org/wiki/Laura_Antonelli
33 https://en.wikipedia.org/wiki/Claude_Lelouch
34 https://en.wikipedia.org/wiki/Costa-Gavras
35 https://en.wikipedia.org/wiki/Gillo_Pontecorvo
36 https://en.wikipedia.org/wiki/Sterling_Hayden

37 https://en.wikipedia.org/wiki/Kirk_Douglas
38 https://en.wikipedia.org/wiki/Peter_Sellers
39 https://en.wikipedia.org/wiki/Michelangelo
40 https://en.wikipedia.org/wiki/Arthur_Rubinstein
41 https://en.wikipedia.org/wiki/Hank_Aaron
42 https://en.wikipedia.org/wiki/George_Blanda
43 https://en.wikipedia.org/wiki/William_Makepeace_Thackeray
44 https://en.wikipedia.org/wiki/Ryan_O%27Neal
45 https://en.wikipedia.org/wiki/Thus_Spoke_Zarathustra
46 https://en.wikipedia.org/wiki/Martin_Scorsese
47 https://en.wikipedia.org/wiki/Fred_Weintraub
48 https://en.wikipedia.org/wiki/Bruce_Lee
49 https://en.wikipedia.org/wiki/Ellen_Burstyn
50 https://en.wikipedia.org/wiki/Norman_Mailer
51 https://en.wikipedia.org/wiki/Alice_Faye
52 https://en.wikipedia.org/wiki/Peggy_Lee
53 https://en.wikipedia.org/wiki/Kris_Kristofferson
54 https://en.wikipedia.org/wiki/Robert_Getchell
55 https://en.wikipedia.org/wiki/Robert_Evans
56 https://en.wikipedia.org/wiki/Margaret_Hamilton_(actress)
57 https://en.wikipedia.org/wiki/Quentin_Tarantino
58 https://en.wikipedia.org/wiki/Sharon_Tate
59 https://en.wikipedia.org/wiki/Brad_Pitt
60 https://en.wikipedia.org/wiki/Charles_Manson
61 https://en.wikipedia.org/wiki/Woody_Allen
62 https://en.wikipedia.org/wiki/Zero_Mostel
63 https://en.wikipedia.org/wiki/Jimmy_Hoffa
64 https://en.wikipedia.org/wiki/Joseph_McCarthy
65 https://en.wikipedia.org/wiki/Julius_and_Ethel_Rosenberg
66 https://en.wikipedia.org/wiki/Andrea_Marcovicci
67 https://en.wikipedia.org/wiki/Martin_Ritt
68 https://en.wikipedia.org/wiki/Walter_Bernstein
69 https://en.wikipedia.org/wiki/Diane_Keaton
70 https://en.wikipedia.org/wiki/John_Cassavetes
71 https://en.wikipedia.org/wiki/Dick_Cavett
72 https://en.wikipedia.org/wiki/Ted_Baxter
73 https://en.wikipedia.org/wiki/The_Mary_Tyler_Moore_Show

74 https://en.wikipedia.org/wiki/Dionne_Warwick
75 http://www.personalmanagershalloffame.org/jeff-wald.html
76 https://en.wikipedia.org/wiki/Mister_Kelly%27s
77 https://en.wikipedia.org/wiki/Michael_Jackson
78 https://en.wikipedia.org/wiki/Mort_Sahl
79 https://en.wikipedia.org/wiki/Ronald_Reagan
80 https://en.wikipedia.org/wiki/Walter_Sheridan
81 https://en.wikipedia.org/wiki/Clay_Shaw
82 https://en.wikipedia.org/wiki/Perry_Russo
83 https://en.wikipedia.org/wiki/Lee_Harvey_Oswald

IV. Comparing Notes

John lives in Las Vegas and I on Long Island so our discussions have been over the phone, via email or Facebook messenger. But no matter how we communicated, it was always entertaining and informative. When it was determined that we wanted to do this book, John took it upon himself to copy all of the reviews from the many *LA Magazines* and send them to me. He also dated them, which was so helpful. They were also very enjoyable to read. I asked John if he appreciated going back in time and reading them again.

He said, "Carol, this may sound weird, but I cannot remember having written them. Re-reading them was totally new to me. I can only recall some lines from three films, only because of the enormous feedback afterwards."

"Which films?"

"*Network, Deep Throat and Gatsby.* And it brought back to mind the joy of seeing wonderful movies or wonderful moments in those movies."

"What was one of the best openings of a movie for you, John?"

"To me, there were two. One was *The Philadelphia Story* when Cary Grant[1] shoves Katharine Hepburn after she breaks his golf club. You immediately know this will be a fun film about a marriage gone wrong. The other is Clint Eastwood's[2] *Hereafter,* made long after I stopped being a critic. It opens with a massive tsunami sucking people to their deaths and sucking us into the film. It is one of Eastwood's best, along with *Gran Torino.* It also reminded me of LeLouche because the possible lovers don't meet till the end."

I couldn't help but think that maybe John missed writing movie reviews and said as much to him.

"No, not at all. I miss good movies. I quit being a critic at the magazine in 1979/1980 when I got *Real People* on NBC. And even though I bashed them the hardest, both Neil Simon and Burt Reynolds phoned, urging me to stay. I declined, telling them that I ran out of ways to say it's a piece of shit."

"But let's not forget that you won Emmys for both entertainment and news shows. So that sort of leads to my next question. What would you consider to be the most important film made?"3

"Carol, a great film entertains and or informs a society. An important film improves society. Only two I know of that have done that. First, *The Jazz Singer* because it introduced sound and the reality of people talking. Second, is Oliver Stone's *JFK,* which moved Congress, forced by the public, to pass The JFK Assassination Records Act[3], calling for the CIA to release all their files 25 years after the October 26, 1992 date of enactment, which they declined to do and with President Trump agreeing. But to me, quite humbly and honestly, although undistributed and unbroadcast but seen by thousands on Amazon and iTunes, the most important film ever made in America is *The American Media and the 2nd Assassination of*

John F. Kennedy. To see it is to know why it's never been on TV. Edward R. Murrow, America's one true muckraking journalist, said TV could improve the world, instead it polluted it with celebrities and stupidity, which is the same thing. Films and TV could have done what books once did: Improve our country. 100 years ago, Upton Sinclair[4] wrote *The Jungle*, which led to the Pure Food Act. In the 50's, Rachel Carson[5] wrote *Silent Spring*, making us aware of DDT and how it pollutes our environment."

Even though this is about movies, John's comments made me think about books, or rather important books. It seems as though books have so much to compete with and yet many that are on the bestseller list offer little more than guilty or not-so-guilty pleasure. As a writer with several published books, I understand the challenges we authors have to get any attention for our books and, in turn, readers.

But speaking of competition, John says, "Having spent my professional life in and having had a love for early TV, which I no longer have, I'm reminded of what Gary Deeb, America's best TV critic at *The Chicago Tribune*[6] said, "TV is the only business in America where competition does not improve the product."

Gary Deeb. He's the one who dubbed John *The* Godfather of Reality TV.

However, since I titled this chapter "Comparing Notes," I thought it would be fun to read some of John's reviews of movies that I was familiar with, and in no particular order. Therefore, in going through the stacks of reviews he'd sent me, the first will be *American Graffiti*. I may have seen this movie more than once in the theater when it first came out. I liked it that much and found that there was so much to digest from it that it deserved more than one viewing. I'm not sure what first drew me to see that particular movie, but it had a great cast, including Ron Howard[7] who has always been a favorite of mine, from when he played Opie on *The Andy Griffith Show*, not to mention the little boy in the movie, *The Courtship of Eddie's Father*, starring Glenn Ford[8]. Odd enough, I wasn't a huge fan of *Happy Days* where he played Richie Cunningham, and yet I liked him as Steve Bolander in *American Graffiti*. I was never a fan of movies where the drama felt manufactured or forced, which is why I enjoyed *American Graffiti*. Let's see if John enjoyed it as well.

An Elegy for the Wet Heads

By John Barbour

The oldies aren't the only golden thing about American Graffiti

Since I knew beforehand that *American Graffiti* dealt with lifestyles and music of the early '60s, I was hoping I'd dislike it. With all the bad plays and films out about America's recent past I've grown to despise manufactured nostalgia. I am tired of seeing the way the Wet Heads parted their hair being treated as though it had all the import of the parting of the Red Sea. I'm tired of TV commercials hawking the Golden Oldies of last May.

I tell you all this upfront so you'll know that for me it would take a hell of a film to justify yet another dredging up of the day before yesterday.

American Graffiti is a hell of a film.

The story takes place one night in 1962, the night before one of the four teenage boys in the film is to leave for college. Their preoccupation is with cars and girls, and the bodywork of both is on display at their soda fountain of youth: Mel's Burger Drive-In. Their guru is the constant rasping, shouting presence of the songs and sounds of disc jockey Wolfman Jack[9].

One of the fellows can barely get through the evening, let along life. In his friend's borrowed car he picks up a boozer who thinks she looks like Sandra Dee[10]. (Maybe that's why she's a boozer.) Because he's too young to buy some liquor himself he has to ask a stranger to buy it for him. The stranger turns out to be a hold-up man. Later, while he's in the bushes with the boozer and the bottle, the car is stolen. When he finds the thieves they admit to it by punching him out.

The way each one of the boys spends his evening is treated episodically, but blended together, there is a remarkable overall substance; credit for this must go to director and co-author George Lucas[11], whose only previous film was an eerie and excellent look at the future: THX 1138 (which turns up here as the license plate on a hotrod.)

I liked the film not only for its painfully evocative treatment of the pre-assassination '60s, but because of the way it brought the characters up to date: still shots are projected of the four boys in the film, letting us know what became of them. One is selling insurance; one died in a car crash; another died in Vietnam, and the last is living in Canada. It's a very simple, effective device that helps to broaden a very simple yet immensely effective film.

Another reason I liked *American Graffiti*: when I got out, my 1963 Studebaker looked like a new car.

So there you have it. John and I are in agreement on that film. I don't think I realized that THX 1138 was a movie, George Lucas's debut and, in turn, didn't catch the relevancy of the license plate. That's what makes going to the movies fun, though, when we feel like we're being treated to a secret that we, the audience, are in on.

I was in high school in 1972 when *Lady Sings the Blues* came out and I couldn't wait to see it. I was a fan of Diana Ross[12] and eager to see her in the role of Billie Holiday[13]. I wasn't disappointed and not long after, I purchased some Billie Holiday albums. But more importantly, I learned more about the Black person's struggles than I ever truly realized. See, I grew up in a rural town where there were no people of color. None. However, it was another movie, one that was made in 1959, that gave me insight on how my parents felt about people whose skin color was different from ours. The movie was *Imitation of Life*, starring Lana Turner[14], Sandra Dee, Juanita Moore[15], Susan Kohner[16], John Gavin[17] and others. There was an earlier version, but I'm quite sure it was the 1959 version that my family and I watched together in our living room. The thing is, my father thought watching TV was a waste of time. He'd only watch Walter Cronkite[18] for the half hour of news weeknights. (I dare say we got more actual news in that half hour than what we now get from 24-hour cable news.) But I digress. Anyway, it was odd to have my father sitting there with us, all of us except my older teenage brother who was outside futzing around, but just like us my father was riveted by the story and none of us had a dry eye when toward the end Mahalia Jackson[19] was singing at Annie Johnson's (Moore) funeral and then watching Annie's daughter (Kohner) screaming, breaking through the crowd, regretting that she had disowned her Black mother since she was able to pass as white due to how light her skin was. That's when my brother walked in and made a joke about us crying. My father turned around in his swivel rocker, his face filled with fury, and yelled at my brother. I don't recall what my father actually said, but it was as though he were scolding my brother for not understanding something important we were witnessing. Yes, it was "just" a movie, but one with a very real message that stuck with me to this day. (As an aside, my father who was a staunch Republican all his life, voted for Barack Obama[20] because he said it was about time a Black person got a chance. I voted for Obama, too, but it wasn't because of his skin color. My father died four years after that election.)

So years later, *Lady Sings the Blues* also had a strong impact on me. And, I thought Billy Dee Williams[21] was smoking hot and had a crush on him. For weeks after I saw the movie, I would "sing" *God Bless the Child* while recalling numerous heartbreaking scenes. However, let's see what John thought.

"Lady" triumphs over despair...

By John Barbour

Traditionally, Hollywood musical biographies bear about the same relationship to their source as chiropractors do to surgery: they just touch the surface. Moreover the implementation of the songs in these musical biographies is generally as self-conscious and awkward as a hole in your sock. Paramount Pictures, though, has just made up for a lot of that with *Lady Sings the Blues*, the biography of Billie Holiday.

Director Sidney J. Furie[22] and writers Terence McCloy[23], Chris Clark[24] and Suzanne De Passe[25] have created a film that nearly equals what Billie Holiday herself created in song; the film is intelligent, moving, and sometimes daring. Moreover, the songs in *Lady Sings the Blues* are not there just because Billie made them famous, but because each of them represents a musical extension cord into her character, revealing something about how she feels and what she thinks.

In that respect, there is one song included which could have shattered the mood director Furie so artfully building, but which instead became a moment of incredible impact.

Traveling with a white band through the South, Billie (perfectly played, as it turns out, by Diana Ross) has them stop on an untraveled country road so she can climb a hill and relieve herself. Atop the hill, behind some bushes, she finds a young black man hanging from a tree, the victim of a lynching. Back in the bus, she says nothing. The camera moves in on her sitting by the window, the hill fading into the moving background, some vague reflections on the glass. Furie lingers on this shot for a while until you get the uneasy feeling you are going to hear her sing, and you think "My God, not a song!" Then softly, over the image on the screen, you hear the haunting lyrics of *Bitter Fruit** and that languid, delicate protest song suddenly invests the scene with a dramatic scope and insight that transcends what we see and hear.

The subject of race is handled throughout the film, in fact, with a sense of daring—in that it is hardly even mentioned. Furie wants us to get to know Billie Holiday as a woman, not a black woman. When she says nothing about the lynching, and later when she is rammed in the face with a pole bearing an American flag by a mob of hooded Klansmen[26], and at other times when neither she nor any other black questions the mentality of that kind of behavior, Furie does two important and necessary things as a craftsman: he draws us closer to her as a human being, and he moves us to ask certain questions on her behalf.

In handling this aspect of the film with restraint and subtlety, he treats the audience with a respect and an intelligence that is as remarkable as it is rare. The less he shows, the more one understands. And in the final scene when Billie is standing, arms uplifted, on the stage of Carnegie Hall, and we know she is going to die, we too are paradoxically uplifted because for the entirety of this movie we have grown to feel for, root for, and laugh with the talented, scrawny girl who grew up in Harlem brothels, possessing only a drive to express herself in music…this woman who would end up dead at 44, an alcoholic and a junkie who could never quite get more than a heartbeat ahead in the painful game of living.

The songs, handled surprisingly well by Diana Ross (after all, there was only one Lady Day), sound as contemporary as Bacharach[27] and the Beatles[28], and the score by Michel Legrand[29] brilliantly reproduces the distinct flavor of the times. Billy Dee Williams as the man who loves Billie, and Richard Pryor[30] as the piano player who discovers her, are excellent, as is everyone else.

I was confused when John referenced *Strange Fruit* as *Bitter Fruit* in his review and wondered if anyone called him out on it, but in my research I found this explanation for the confusion:

*It was named the song of the century by *Time* magazine in 1999, and the story of *Strange Fruit*'s conception has entered legend. Originally a poem called *Bitter Fruit*, it was written by the Jewish school teacher Abel Meeropol under the pseudonym Lewis Allen in response to lynching in US southern states.

Only recently, Hulu streamed *The United States vs. Billie Holiday* starring Andra Day[31]. And what I learned from that movie that I don't recall seeing in *Lady Sings the Blues* is how the FBI threatened Billie Holiday if she performed *Strange Fruit*, saying it was incendiary. Talk about infuriating—the subject matter of the song wasn't the issue for the FBI but rather the response to it. Our country has many sins and those lynchings must be tragically counted as one of them. Sadly, there's still racism, which became even more apparent when only recently there were several nooses found on a construction site. This is why making important movies can shine a light on the hatred that exists in hopes of educating the haters and apathetic so we can make a change for the better as a society.

It's fair to say that John and I don't agree on all the movies we've both seen.

One is *A Star is Born*. No, I'm not referring to the latest remake starring Bradley Cooper[32] and Lady Gaga,[33] nor the Judy Garland[34] and James Mason[35] 1954 version or even the 1937 rendition with Janet Gaynor[36] and Fredric March[37], but the one from 1976 with Barbra Streisand[38] and Kris Kristofferson. But first, let's read what John thought.

Each remake of *A Star is Born* gets a little more diluted: the latest version starring Barbra Streisand and Kris Kristofferson, has as much relationship to the original as Hawaiian Punch has to champagne. In fact, the film's story line has gone the route of the second "a" in Barbra—it's been thrown out and replaced with a song.

It's impossible for a film in which Streisand sings not to have some good moments, but the excessive showcasing of her vocal skills at the expense of the script and character relationships makes *A Star is Born* look not like a movie so much as her next album cover—with less to it than meets the ears. In spite of the considerable presence and talent of both Streisand and Kristofferson, the characters they portray have no character.

Kristofferson plays John Norman Howard, a raunchy rock star who loves drinking booze, snorting coke, picking fights and accommodating groupies; what he hates are success and himself. He stumbles around sullenly without anybody ever knowing why he's such a mess. One night he stumbles into a club where Streisand, as Esther Hoffman, is working as a singer. After starting a scuffle with another patron that "blows" Esther's act as well as wrecking the club, he is spared more headlines when she leads him out a back door. A couple of days later, he's so in love with her he wants her to have his career.

In order to believe this you're going to have to be more than stoned; you're going to have to be stupid. He hands his career to her a few nights later at a benefit concert for some Indians; over the protestations of the crowd, which has come to hear *him*, he introduces Esther. Her song here makes her an instant star. And rightly so, because the way Streisand sings, this song—and an earlier scene at an outdoor rock concert, during which Kristofferson spills off the stage on a motorcycle—are the only naturally high points in the film.

To say that after Esther becomes a star the film goes downhill is misleading because it never quite went uphill. From here on it just stagnates. And since Streisand's name is in the credits almost as much as her face is on the screen, she had to take the blame—or the credit—for everything, including one unflattering shot of her in a bathtub with Kristofferson that looks more like he's in there with Harpo Marx[39].

The music from *A Star is Born* may make a good LP, but as a film, *A Star* is boring.

One point John makes that I agree with is that *A Star is Born* made a great LP[40]. Similar to what I did after seeing *Lady Sings the Blues*, I went out and bought myself a copy and blasted it almost daily. I may have even gone to the theater more than once to watch the movie, especially since I was and am a fan of both Streisand and Kristofferson.

Readers may be familiar with the Judy Garland version that airs at least once a year on Turner Classic Movies where scenes were lost while the soundtrack was found. Therefore, still photos are used to replace those missing scenes, making it feel like an awkward intermission.

I'd asked John if he'd seen the Lady Gaga and Bradley Cooper version and he gave me a single word reply, "No." Had he watched it he might have appreciated the fact that the characters were more developed, something he felt was lacking in the '76 version. I had little intention of seeing it, however, after my adult kids raved about it and continuously played the song *Shallow*, (But how could that tune upstage *Evergreen*?) I agreed to go. It did keep a similar storyline and I do like both Gaga and Cooper as performers, but I still preferred Streisand and Kristofferson. I believe I'm in the minority, though, and would be curious to know what John would think if he ever decides to watch it. But the idea of remakes led me to ask John what he thought of them overall.

He said, "No remake has ever had more impact than the original. And in the '50's, comedian Fred Allen[41] said of remakes: 'Hollywood is like a swarm of termites constantly chewing on their own backlog!' Articulate… and brilliant!"

Okay, so John only recently learned this about me: I used to be a born-again Christian. In 1974 I "came to the Lord" but a few years later, came to my senses. I was sincere in my stance then and just as sincere where I stand now. There's no need for me to go into further explanation here but the reason I bring it up is reading John's movie review of *The Hiding Place*, which was initially a book by Corrie ten Boom[42]. I was so inspired by Corrie ten Boom that I named my first daughter Corrie. The movie came out in 1975, right when I was an active member of a Baptist church.

Jeannette Clift[43] played the part of Corrie and Julie Harris[44], her sister, Betsie.

John makes no secret of the fact that he doesn't believe in any God or religion so I was curious how he reviewed this one. Let's give it a look:

It's Billy Graham's Hiding Place that's the mongrel[45]

One of the lines in the ad promoting the film *The Hiding Place* says: "The story that thrilled 6 million is now a motion picture." Since "6 million" has also come to mean the number of Jews who perished in death camps, I feel using that figure in the ad was unfortunate—and unsettling. And that was the reaction I had to the movie.

The Hiding Place is based on the true story of a Dutch-Christian family named Ten Boom that gave refuge to Jews during the German occupation. But while the story is true, in the hands of Billy Graham's filmmakers, the treatment is unfortunate. Here, truth is not stranger than fiction—it's just duller. For the first tedious hour all the members of this family, while trying to figure a way to hide the Jews in their home, walk around in a euphoric fog saying that God will provide. That may be true, but what God didn't provide was a writer and, most importantly, a director.

For this first hour we are almost always inside the house, and not once do we feel the horror or the terror of what is going on outside. At times, you get the feeling that perhaps Graham's people didn't want to show (or admit) such horrors could exist; then you realize the director was simply incapable of capturing them. One example is a scene in which the family and the refugees are planning to build a brick wall in the house behind which the refugees can hide. The bricks are being brought in encased in a grandfather clock, and when the guys carrying the clock get inside, they are stopped by a German soldier whose fascination with clocks had been set up in an earlier scene. Now, this moment could have held quite a bit of tension had the audience known beforehand that the soldier was already inside—but since this was *not* known, the moment lay there like a ton of bricks.

Julie Harris and Eileen Heckart[46] do their best as members of the Ten Boom family, but Arthur O'Connell[47] as the father treats the refugees as if they were kids coming in for a tube of Crest.

I think I'll keep the religious theme going and take a look at 1973's *Jesus Christ Superstar*. I believe this was the beginning of my search for meaning in my life and convinced my mother to bring me to see the movie. My mom, a born again Christian, was amenable to the idea and I suppose she felt it would be a good way to teach me about the ways of the Lord. (Turns out, I taught her a couple of things from the Bible that she hadn't known, even though she'd gone to Sunday School most of her life.) After seeing the movie, I asked for the album for Christmas and got it. *Hosanna hey sanna sanna sanna ho Sanna hey sanna hosanna* poured from my bedroom day and night. I liked the Jesus in this movie. Not only was he cute, he was a rebel, although during the scene when he overturned the moneychanger's tables in the temple, my mother thought that was just drama for the movie, until I corrected her, telling her according to Matthew 21: 12-13 and Mark 11:15-18, that's exactly what he'd done. Turns out that beatific-looking Jesus in the picture hanging in our kitchen had a temper.

Now, anyone who's read John's memoir, knows that he gave religion a chance, as well, until he discovered that prayers weren't always answered the way he'd hoped. But did *Jesus Christ Superstar* bring him into the fold?

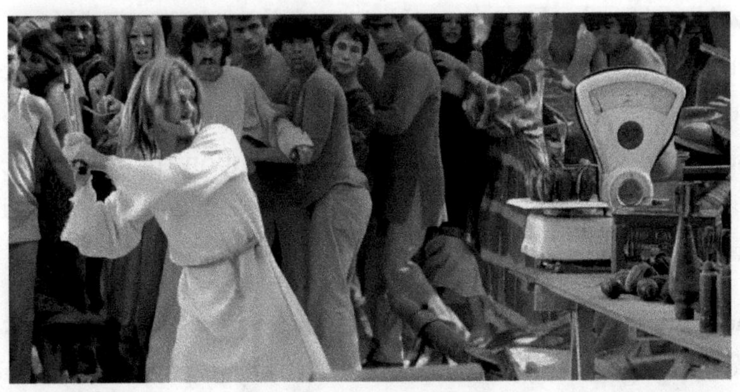

...And so Jewison brought forth four tanks, two jets, one machine—everything but a partridge in a pear tree

In the beginning there was the play, *Jesus Christ Superstar*. It was full of wonderful music and vitality and Universal Pictures looked out over the profits it maketh and said: "That is good. Let there be a movie." But the movie was without a director and so Universal looked over *Fiddler on the Roof* and the profits it maketh and said: "That is good. Let Norman Jewison[48] be the director." And so it was.

But the movie was without a writer, so Jewison said: "Let me be one of the writers." And so he made himself a writer and lo, the movie was still without a writer.

And the director-writer was without ideas and lo, he looked again upon *Fiddler* and said: "I have an idea. I will go on location to the Holy Land and do *Fiddler on the Mount* in the Land of the Profits." It was a bad idea.

And so the talented cast was assembled in the wilderness and for 40 days and 40 nights wandered without direction, and when Jewison looked upon the daily rushes, which were without form and void of imagination, verily he said unto himself: "Whatta I do now?"

And a voice from the Darkness (Universal Tower) sayeth: "How about some symbolism?" And so Jewison brought forth four tanks, two jets, one machine—everything but a partridge in a pear tree. And the symbolism was obscure. And when Jewison looked again upon the rushes, he said, "I have another idea! To keep the audiences awake, let there be decibels." And verily, the beautiful music was made loud noise: another bad idea.

And when Universal Publicity looked upon Jewison's finished work, they said: "Yea, it is good." Because that's what they're paid to say. But yea, verily and lo, when the audience looks up *Jesus Christ Superstar*, it will say: "Forgive them, for they know not what they do."

I admit, I couldn't stop laughing as I copied the review from *LA Magazine* while also thinking that only someone who studied the Bible could have written such a witty commentary. Did it change my mind about the movie? Not at all, since I did enjoy the music. But it's also true that *Jesus Christ Superstar* didn't win neither John nor myself back into any fold.

The same year that *Jesus Christ Superstar* came out in the theater was when the off-Broadway musical, *Godspell*, was adapted to film. So when I wasn't singing *I Don't Know How to Love Him* from *JC Superstar*, I was singing *Day By Day*. Again, when I say "singing," I don't want to give the impression that I have any musical talent because I do not. Anyway, John had a number of reviews in brief and *Godspell* was one of them. He wrote:

To some traditionalists, Jesus in a Superman shirt may not be their cup of testament, but it's hard to remember a musical more imaginatively translated to the screen. Future generations of kids may say of this exuberant and moving musical *Godspell* according to St. Matthew, "Upon this rock..."

I think it's fair to say that in 1977 Steven Spielberg had proven himself as a talent who could bring patrons into the theater in droves. Case in point: *Close Encounters of the Third Kind.* Spielberg put together an amazing cast, including Richard Dreyfuss, Melinda Dillon[49], Teri Garr[50] and Bob Balaban[51]. I appreciated this movie because of what it didn't show. We as the audience know that something powerful is at play and wreaking havoc with Dreyfuss's character without having things, such as creepy aliens, go boo in the night. The drama was in the unknown while leaving hints throughout. Okay, so I'm not a talented reviewer like John, so I'll let him take over from his December 1977 review:

Close Encounters: Bewitching Oz for Adults

By John Barbour

That Spielberg's a whiz of a wiz!

Within a week of the opening of *Star Wars* there were almost as many people rushing to stand in line to buy 20th Century-Fox stock as there were rushing to stand in line to buy tickets. In anticipation of Steven Spielberg's *Close Encounters of the Third Kind* being another box office stockbuster, weeks before its opening people were calling their brokers saying, "Please, Paine Webber[52], buy me Columbia shares!"

Now that *Close Encounters* has opened I don't know if those people will have the occasion to say, "Thanks, Paine Webber." It does not have R2D2, Darth Vader, C3PO, or any of the other merchandising potential of *Star Wars*, so Columbia's stock may not go up much more than it already has. However, after seeing this absolutely magnificent Julia[53] and Michael Phillips[54] production, there is no doubt that Spielberg's stock as America's most inspired, original and gifted filmmaker will skyrocket. He is Stanley Kubrick with soul. Compared to this, *Star Wars* is a Tinkertoy[55].

The first scene is set in a Mexican desert during a sandstorm. Francois Truffaut as a scientist doing research into UFOs and some U.S. military personnel have been brought to this spot by an incredible discovery: Following the appearance of a blinding midnight light which seared his face and almost rendered him imbecilic, an aging peasant recovered to find, intact, five U.S. fighter planes that had mysteriously disappeared 32 years earlier over the Bermuda Triangle.[56] From this opening scene, our imagination is swept up, and Spielberg's storytelling and filmmaking artistry takes us on a wonderfully entertaining, almost spiritual journey down a metaphysical yellow brick road. *Close Encounters* is *The Wizard of Oz* for adults!

Richard Dreyfuss plays a power-company employee who finds himself fired from his job, estranged from his wife and family—and almost from his sanity—by his obsession with tracking the source of the mysterious blinding light, apparently a UFO. And he is superb. In his quest he encounters Melinda Dillon, whose young son mysteriously disappears after the object hovers outside her house—which is almost torn apart by its presence.

The U.S. military and Truffaut eventually make contact with the UFO by the transmission of what are musical notes—actually the language of the interplanetary visitors. They then prepare secretly to make actual contact at a remote, quarantined spot in Wyoming. Meanwhile, Dreyfuss, Dillon, the old Mexican peasant and a few others who have had contact with the object are drawn to this spot almost telepathically.

Douglas Trumball's[57] special effects are phenomenal: John Williams'[58] music does for the ear what Vilmos Zsigmond's[59] glorious photography does for the eye. And in the last half hour Spielberg brings his story together in some emotionally and intellectually stirring moments that are filmmaking magic at its joyous best.

Not many people could afford to buy Columbia stock, but no one can afford to miss buying a ticket to *Close Encounters*. Besides, the real profit is in seeing it.

Here's the thing as I read John's review: I had no memory of that opening scene. What I did recall was the recognizable music and the sand piles that Dreyfuss was obsessed to build. Now I am determined to watch the movie once again. Why? John's review, of course.

I had a history teacher, Mr. Wilson, in high school who was riveted by the whole Watergate[60] break-in and Nixon's resignation. I'm not sure if he was supposed to be teaching other topics but, if so, he would skim them and then go on and on about how our country's democracy was compromised. (I can only imagine what he'd be thinking about today's politics.) Anyway, I do give Mr. Wilson credit for getting me somewhat interested in politics back then, an interest that has grown over the years. So, a few years later, 1976 as a matter of fact, after I'd graduated and began my life as a bonafide adult, I eagerly bought a ticket for *All the President's Men,* which was based on the book with the same title by Carl Bernstein[61] and Bob Woodward[62], and watched history unfold on the big screen. (Years later, when I worked as a National Events Coordinator for Borders Books, Park Avenue, Manhattan, Carl Bernstein attended one of the events I was hosting. I don't recall who the event was for, but remember finding it stunning to be in the same room with such a notable reporter. Any conversation I had with him was no more than a hello and goodnight. I may have thrown in, "Thank you for coming.")

Anyway, I thoroughly enjoyed the movie and felt almost as riveted by the events as my history teacher was years earlier. I wonder how riveted John was.

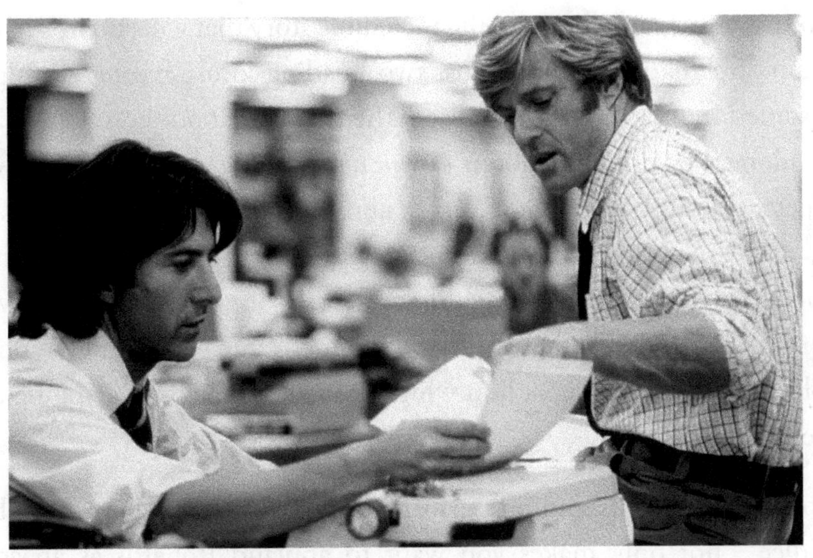

Remembering the Good Old Days with All the Editor's Men

By John Barbour

Chalk one up for Woodredfordstein

In the opening sequence, the theater screen is entirely white; then, in microscopic close-up, we see typewriter keys begin to smash slowly onto the paper, filling the screen with the sight of each individual letter. Thus director Alan Pakula begins *All the President's Men*—an impressive film starring Robert Redford and Dustin Hoffman—with an awesome reminder of the impact, power and importance of the printed word in a free press. And one of the *most* impressive things about it is its low-key, almost dramatic documentary approach to how the *Washington Post* and reporters Bob Woodward and Carl Bernstein pursued the Watergate break-in.

Hoffman and Redford, who were never better, do not at first give the impression they may be on to the incredible story that will end in Richard Nixon's resignation; they are just two hustling local reporters trying to do something for their own careers. The film isn't about how a President is undone, but primarily about how a newspaper is put together—with its petty jealousies, irreverent humor and inspired professionalism. With this as a backdrop to the underplayed tedium and excitement of how Woodward and Bernstein track down leads, counterpointed with what the audience knows is the eventual outcome. Pakula and writer William Goldman[63] have created a film which manages to be both gripping and utterly honest.

Jason Robards' outstanding performance as *Post* executive editor Ben Bradlee[64] not only makes you want to applaud Robards as an actor but Bradlee as a newspaperman. And Hal Holbrook[65] is hauntingly magnificent as the informant, Deep Throat, whose voice from the darkness hints at even greater darknesses.

The one flaw is the film's end. After getting us involved with the two reporters for over two years of time and two hours of film, and after leading us to expect to see actual news footage of Nixon's resignation, all we're shown is the teletype keys spelling it all out. And, what's worse, we see absolutely no reaction from the two reporters whose story may have caused it all.

Other than that, *All the President's Men* is the kind of a film to make all of us feel the pride and pain that comes with having a free press.

I'm not sure that I agree with John regarding that ending. I often believe that less is more and ending the film the same way as it opened with typewriter keys feels right to me. (As a side note, sadly and tragically, Alan Pakula died in 1998 on the Long Island Expressway when a car in front of him struck a metal pipe. The pipe went through Pakula's windshield and caused him to swerve off the road. He died instantly.) Anyway, if you're reading this and haven't seen *All the President's Men* yet, I hope you make a point to watch it. It brings history to life.

As a young woman and quasi-feminist, I was eager to see *Lipstick*, which also came out in 1976. (I say "quasi" because I also was in the throes of living the born-again Christian life and tried to do what was being taught, AKA being brainwashed, and honor my husband no matter what.) I knew the subject matter of *Lipstick* was about rape and two sisters, played by the actual sisters, Margaux Hemingway[66] and Mariel Hemingway[67], granddaughters of the famous writer, Ernest Hemingway[68]. For some reason, I was intrigued and went to see the movie. I think I found it cheesy and yet still rooted for the rapist to get his just desserts. Roger Ebert said *Lipstick* was "a nasty little item masquerading as a bold statement on the crime of rape. The statement would seem a little bolder if the movie didn't linger in violent and graphic detail over the rape itself, and then handle the vengeance almost as an afterthought."

Let's find out if John agreed.

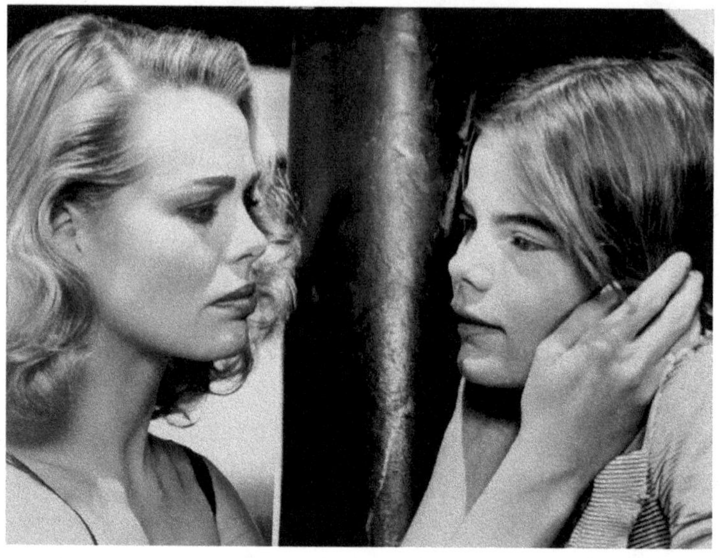

In every movie I've seen in which a woman is raped—including last year's *Death Wish* with Charles Bronson[69]—it was always the husband, brother, father or boyfriend who sought revenge. Well, with the increase in the number of rapes and the increase in women's awareness in general, it was only a matter of time before somebody would make a film in which the violated woman extracts her *own* revenge. That film is *Lipstick*, and the desire to exploit rather than explore seems to be the only motivation for making a movie that is no more than *Death Wish in Drag*.

Margaux Hemingway is a 6-foot-tall model who plays a 6-foot-tall model whose ads for a lipstick are smeared all over the city. Her kid sister (played by the real-life kid sister) introduces Margaux to the rapist—a music teacher from her all-girls' Catholic school, played by Chris Sarandon[70], with about as much authority as a nude policeman trying to direct rush-hour traffic. From the very beginning, the film goes for the obvious and the groin, and never relents in this dedication.

The grislies begin as Sarandon brings a recording of one of his compositions to Margaux's apartment, at her invitation. However, when she stops listening to answer the phone, he tries to get her attention again by raping her in a scene as excessively repulsive as the crime. Eventually, Sarandon goes to trial, but is acquitted; discouraged, Margaux decides to take her kid sister to the mountains on a hunting trip, stopping for a moment at the Pacific Design Center on Melrose, that blue building that looks like it manufactures Tidy Bowl. And while the kid sister is waiting, it's *her* turn to be raped by the teacher.

The fact that much of the audience cheers when Margaux goes hunting in the parking lot means many are seduced by the film's theme. In actuality they've merely been mentally raped by its shallowness.

Mentally raped. I would have to agree with that. However, Mariel, who was fourteen at the time, was nominated for a Golden Globe and went on to perform in *Manhattan* with Woody Allen. Sadly, Margaux died much too young of a drug overdose.

While working on this book, Dr. Aaron Stern[71] passed away. You may wonder why I'd mention what seems like a non sequitur. As it happens, Dr. Stern was director of movie ratings in the '70s. According to his obituary in *The New York Times*, Dr. Stern, a psychiatrist, was the "head of Hollywood's movie rating board in the early 1970s and established himself as a kind of filmgoers' sentry against carnal imagery and violence." This news led me to ask John what he thought of that movie rating system.

John said, "I do not think anyone or any entity should be determining what people should see or read. But since reading is private, but film viewing a group activity, I think they handled the film ratings sensibly…from G, PG, R and X. And X rated *Deep Throat* did as well as G rated *The Sound of Music*!"

I've always been a sucker for movies where dancing was a theme, but it's not like I had any training in dancing since I grew up on a farm in Upstate New York. There were no studios within a forty-mile radius. And even if there were, it's certain my parents wouldn't have thought my going to take dance lessons was worth the time or money. So, I used to try to catch American Bandstand and Soul Train to watch the latest dance crazes and practice in my living room. Then when I moved to Long Island, the first Broadway show I went to was *A Chorus Line*. But on the big screen in 1977, there was the hit *Saturday Night Fever* starring John Travolta[72] where disco was the rage. I wasn't a fan of John Travolta's, although I did like him in *The Boy in the Plastic Bubble*, which was based on a true story, and where we get a hint of Travolta's dance moves. I don't recall loving *Saturday Night Fever* as much as I enjoyed the soundtrack, which brought the Bee Gees[73] renewed fame. It wasn't until 1983 when I saw *Flashdance* that I related to the character's desire to dance. I went back two more times to watch that movie, eager to see that close to last scene where Alex Owen, played by Jennifer Beals[74], auditions for the ballet. (I found out later that Beals had body doubles for those inspirational dances.) And then a year later, I went to see *Footloose* and found myself bopping, tapping and rooting for Ren (played by Kevin Bacon[75]) as he tried to get the town ordinance changed to allow for dancing.

As it happens, John didn't review *Flashdance* or *Footloose*, but he did review *Saturday Night Fever* and provided some interesting backstory:

As I Was Saying Before I Was So Rudely Interrupted…

By John Barbour

Fearless notes from a critic in exile

I am writing this in Chicago. After doing reviews or talk shows at almost every station in Los Angeles, and at some of them twice, I am now using up other cities. I have been signed for five weeks to host *A.M. Chicago* at WLS-TV, the ABC outlet here, and to appear three times a week on the 6 o'clock news as a critic. The nice thing about this job is that I knew how brief my stay would be *before* I was hired.

The previous host-critic, Steve Edwards[76], was hired away by L.A.'s own KNXT primarily to do the weather—at something like $175,000 a year. Occasionally during a forecast, I understand, Steve clutches his chest like Dr. George, but only because that's where he keeps his wallet.

I am here because, shortly after leaving KNBC in December, I got a call from WLS's general manager, Phil Boyer[77], who used to be the KNBC program director when I was a critic-not-quite-this-far-at-large. He told me that for a few weeks over the holidays and New Year's, while they were looking for a good, permanent host, they needed a good, temporary host. Having worked with me in the past, Phil knew how temporary I could be.

I always thought it would be nice to be seen in Chicago, but not in person. Especially in the winter. Ten years ago, in December, I was Dionne Warwick's opening act at Mr. Kelly's on Rush Street. The day we opened they found a polar bear frozen to death in Lincoln Park Zoo. They said it was a heart attack. I think he read the thermometer and committed suicide. Mr. Kelly's is gone now, but the zoo has a new polar bear. Chicago knows what the public wants.

One year after the death of Mayor Daley[78], it's still true that if you die a Democrat here you don't lose your right to vote. Since he's been gone I hear he's passed three bills through the city council. And then there are the cops: In the last few weeks three of them hijacked an armored car that was picking up the receipts from highway toll booths and another was caught stealing cars, claiming that he just towed them away a couple of months ago because they were overparked and he had simply forgotten to notify the owners.

Then, two weeks ago, a rookie cop who had been drinking pulled a guy off the downtown subway train and shot him. This cop may have been conducting the Chicago Police Department's sobriety test—where an officer goes to a local bar, downs four free beers, then goes out and stops the first civilian and makes the guy walk a straight line while he takes target practice. When I learned the officer was only suspended I could almost hear our own Chief Davis singing, "Chicago is…my kind of town!"

On New Year's Eve five unsuspecting people were hit by stray bullets. Since firecrackers are illegal, some revelers celebrated by shooting off handguns. People were afraid to call the police because they wanted to keep the number of wounded to a minimum. Chicagoans, however, seem to be more bemused than appalled by these antics. A corrupt public servant can provide Chicagoans with almost as much entertainment as any accomplished performer.

As for the Chicagoans themselves, they are outspoken without being rude, friendly without being familiar, and a lively, lusty, practical lot who endorse anybody's efforts to get a bigger hunk of cheese in the American rat race. They will support and applaud anything or anybody as long as it's the best or the biggest, be it a crook, the Sears Tower, a drunk, a steak, a financier, a movie star, a call girl or a brain surgeon.

The first week I was here I got an insight into the Chicago psyche. It was in a rest room. After the fellow at the urinal had finished, he retrieved a paper towel from the dispenser, and instead of wiping his hands, he wiped his shoes. This had nothing to do with the fact that there is a large Polish population here. Being practical, he wanted to save his best shoes, which were worth more than the cheap soap.

The two best and therefore most watched TV news shows are on WBBM, the CBS affiliate, and on my temporary home, WLS—whose approach is remarkably similar to that on my former *home*, KNBC. If ABC News' happy talk originated here, it moved to Los Angeles long ago. The three very professional and personable anchormen on WLS have names like Flynn, Daly and Drury. Two of the black field reporters are also Irish.

Chicago's version of KNXT is the NBC affiliate, WMAQ. The set looks as if the Titanic sank, leaving only the ship's control room above water, where the heads of a few survivors can be seen moving about. The face of one of the anchormen, Michael Jackson (no relation to L.A.'s) is so stiff it looks as if he accidentally sprayed *it* instead of his hair. Another guy, Ron Hunter, has so much lacquer on his Beverly Hills casual cut he appears to be wearing a Chicago Bears football helmet.

If the TV news programs, even the good ones, are similar to those in Los Angeles, the newspapers certainly are not. Fifty years ago over morning coffee and evening meals, Chicagoans were reading the literate and irreverent likes of Ben Hecht and Charles MacArthur[79]. It is a tradition this city still subscribes to. The brightest, liveliest newspaper writing in the country is in Chicago's three dailies. Without Jim Murray[80] and Conrad[81] the *Los Angeles Times* would be irredeemably dull. With them it is just redeemably dull.

Now that John Leonard[82] is no longer writing under the name Cyclops, the smartest, most astute TV criticism in America is by Gary Deeb, in the *Chicago Tribune*. Not only do Deeb's columns make for informative, entertaining reading; they often make news.

Much of the sports reporting at the *L.A. Times* is on a level with film and TV criticism, where what passes for reviews looks more like press agentry. Not so with sports reporting in Chicago. When the Los Angeles Kings were here playing the hometown Black Hawks, my wife and son and I were the only three people, of course, cheering for the Kings, but we outnumbered those cheering for the Hawks. It was that kind of game. What a pleasure and surprise it was, the next day, to open the sports page and read an honest and opinionated appraisal in which the reporter said that the Black Hawks and the Kings were *both* outskated by the referees!

Chicagoans, not satisfied with having some of the best writing in the country, demand to have the best in the world. They have that in Chicago *Daily News* columnist Mike Royko[83]. Royko has the genius of a Neil Simon and the social conscience of a Clarence Darrow[84] (another Chicago boy). His typewriter should be enshrined in the Smithsonian. Recently, he wrote: "If God was antihomosexual, why did He choose a gay Michelangelo to paint the Sistine Chapel and Anita Bryant[85] to sell orange juice?" Unfortunately, the *Daily News* is, as of this writing, to be on its last legs—and by the time you read this who knows where Chicagoans will be getting their afternoon Royko fix.

With all the spunky writers scrambling to do columns and sports, this leaves the pedantic to do the film reviews. This also harks back to a tradition—when Carl Sandburg[86] did them for the *Daily News*. Like Sandburg speaking, most of the film critics here huff and puff in print.

With so much red-blooded writing appearing elsewhere, to find film criticism so anemic and academic seemed contrary to the character of Chicago. Then I realized it was actually in keeping with the character of Chicago. To the readers and writers in this city, make-believe is still of much less importance to them than life. Frequently they don't want to know if a movie is good, they want to know if the theater is safe.

My second week here I read three absolutely rave reviews of *Saturday*

Night Fever by three of the most prominent critics. It was then I gave up reading them altogether. In Los Angeles, where most films originate, many critics tend to be producers' groupies; in New York, where they think most ideas originate, many tend to be directors' groupies. In Chicago, where I had expected more independence and originality, I find they are John Travolta groupies. One critic went so far as to say—now get this: "In his first starring film, John Travolta is another Humphrey Bogart and possibly the Fred Astaire[87] of the '70s."

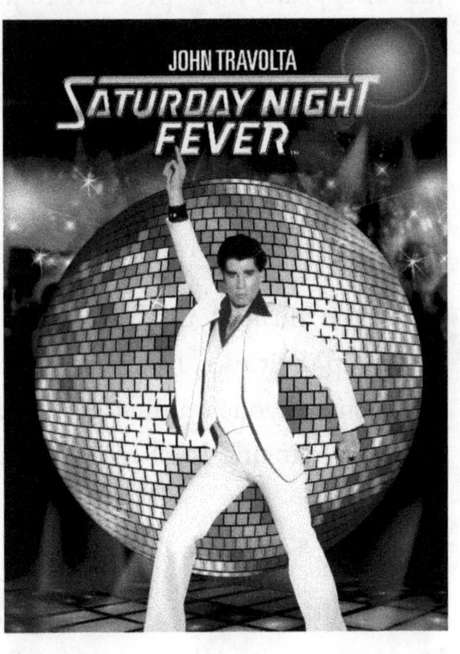

If Travolta is Bogart or Astaire, Son of Sam[88] is Albert Schweitzer[89], and if the author of that is a critic, so is Regis Philbin[90]. What Travolta *is* is a male Farrah Fawcett-Majors[91]—an appealing but manufactured cult figure who makes more appearances on posters than in films.

He is also the only reason for a movie like *Saturday Night Fever* to exist—and not too good a reason at that. In *Welcome Back, Kotter* he plays an engaging slob. In *Fever* he expands his talents: He plays an engaging slob who swears and dances. When his mouth isn't full of profanity, it's full of pizza. His big ambition in the film is to win a Saturday-night dance contest—and he wants to win it with the only girl who doesn't want him to bugaloo all over her body. She wants more out of life. She wants to meet classier people—like Laurence Olivier, who appeared, as she says, in such things as the Polaroid commercial. And the guys Travolta hangs around with in the film are no more than horny sweathogs in what could be called *Dead End Kids Go Disco*, with a plot out of *Beach Blanket Bingo*.

The potentially most interesting characters are barely seen. Travolta's brother is a priest who quits the priesthood because he says he can't live up to his vows of celibacy. After he attends a dance with John, it looks like he quit the movie. At one point, Travolta and his gang mistakenly assault a rival gang, thinking it had been responsible for a sneak attack on one of their buddies. That gang, which is bigger, never retaliates. It just disappears, too—probably to join the priest.

The only amusing moment in the film takes place when Travolta's family gets into an argument around the dinner table, and each one takes a turn punching the one next to him. And the girls in the film are treated so crudely the only way you can tell the difference between the gang wars and the gang bangs is that the latter take place in the back seat of a car.

While the music by the Bee Gees could make even Coroner Naguchi's[92] wards tap their toes, how many times have you actually gone to a disco and seen everyone on the floor doing the same choreographed number? Travolta's dancing is all right, though it wouldn't distract anybody on *Soul Train*.

Travolta *does* reveal that he has the talent and sensitivity to perhaps play something other than a sweathog slob. There is no movie without him, but that's like complimenting a toilet because the handle works.

As most readers will know, John Travolta went on to make quite a number of movies where he was the lead. I suppose due to his success in *Saturday Night Fever*, the following year he starred in *Grease*, and it went on to be a commercial success. I wasn't a fan. The character of Sandy, played by Olivia Newton-John[93], was so sweet it made my teeth ache. I like characters with an edge. Although, I do have a memory of when she appeared in the skin-tight black leather outfit and how my then husband sat up straight in his seat, his eyes bugged out, which, admittedly, was out of character for him. But, back to the movie—I felt it was cheesy and predictable but, again, it was a commercial success, so what do I know? I wonder if John agreed with me.

Grease slips and slides straight downhill

There's only a year and a half left in this decade. Before it runs out, I'd like to go into the theater or turn on the TV and experience more of what art intended us to experience: Present Shock. It's for this reason I must confess that, as a critic, whenever I know I have to review something set in the '50s, I walk into the theater with a chip on my shoulder the size of a redwood.

Seeing *Grease,* with John Travolta and Olivia Newton-John, did not knock that chip off. It only made me conscious of how much weight I was carrying trying to sit through it. There is no doubt that Travolta reveals enough charm to fill the dimple in his chin—in fact the people who like *Grease* will probably be those who think the greatest attribute a human being can have is a hole in his chin.

The film is supposed to be some sort of musical spoof of that generation of teenagers in the '50s who had nothing on their minds but that greasy kid stuff; having been inundated with more of these stories than you can shake a comb at, audiences will find that *Grease* really ends up being mindless. It does not reflect the youth of the '50s and it doesn't communicate to the youth of the '70s. It's in limbo—somewhere between the wethead and the dry look.

Travolta plays a guy who has eyes and hands for Newton-John. When he is together with the gang, though, he has to preserve his macho image. Newton-John has eyes and hands-off for Travolta, and when she is with him she tries to preserve her virginity. Olivia, like John, is pleasant, but in this role it's difficult for her not to come off like an Australian Doris Day. The '70s may be trying to bring back the '50s, but people will never buy bringing back virginity.

What keeps *Grease* from slipping off the screen entirely are some of the dance numbers, which have been choreographed with vitality and imagination. Watching them is like watching the Dallas Cowgirls when the Cowboys are having a bad day. Their enthusiasm and energy are so irresistibly infectious, you almost forget that the rest of the team is losing.

I didn't see *The Goodbye Girl* in the theater. I recall watching it on a lazy Sunday afternoon and glad I didn't spend the money to see it in a theater. Not that I disliked it, but I felt it was a great made-for-TV movie. What bothered me the most was the precocious child played by Quinn Cummings.[94] Not that she didn't play the part well, but in real life I find precocious children obnoxious and in the movies, contrived. But I'm not the critic. John is. Here's his review from 1977:

From John Travolta to Robert Redford, there are quite a few stars whose name on a film is sufficient to sell tickets. There is a selectively smaller handful of directors, from Hitchcock to Spielberg, whose names can do the same. But there is only one writer in that category: Neil Simon.

If Simon had written nothing except *The Goodbye Girl*, that screenplay would be enough to prove that when it comes to writing dialogue, he stands alone. Not only do the lines crackle constantly with wit, but coupled with the enormously vibrant, natural performances of Marsha Mason[95] and Richard Dreyfuss, the movie takes on a quality I haven't seen in American films in 20 years. That quality is grace. At times there is such a gracious glow to the film you get the feelng you could just walk in off the streets and out of the Chicago winter and the screen would warm your hands as well as your heart.

Mason plays a former dancer and divorcee. She has a daughter (wonderfully played by Quinn Cummings) who is so bright that when the parents divorced she must have been given custody of her mother. The two live with an actor—at least they think they do. After going out on a shopping trip to pick up the things they were all supposed to take to California, they come home to find he has taken off in the other direction, to Italy, to make a movie. Mom is so devastated that the daughter has to read her the goodbye note.

Marsha now has to go back to work. She has to get her life in shape, and there are some funny moments watching her as a dancer trying to get her body in shape. Then, just when she figures she can go on living, she finds out it may not be in that apartment. Her former live-in lover had sold the lease to an actor from Chicago (Dreyfuss). The two negotiate strained separate-but-equal living arrangements and, with much difficulty, Dreyfuss moves in.

Dreyfuss has come to New York to play the lead in an off-Broadway production of *Richard III*—his big ambition is to be a big actor. But he is shattered when the director has him playing the part more like a flaming queen than a king, and the play closes after one performance—with all the critics concurring that he played Richard III like the Wicked Witch of the North. One thing does come of it, though: It breaks down the wall between him and Mason—who not only disliked him personally but vowed never to get involved with another actor.

Unfortunately, the closing moments in *Goodbye Girl* seem contrived and artificial, as Simon forces some last-minute manufactured conflict into the script in an effort to raise some doubts as to whether or not the two really will stay together. A less obvious and more bittersweet but hopeful ending would have been more in keeping with the mood, characters and story Simon had created.

But even if the story ends before the film, the charm does not. And there is nothing more honest than the enjoyment you will experience if you *do* go to a theater and say hello to Neil Simon's *The Goodbye Girl.*

Okay, so John was far more tolerant of a precocious child than I was. Also, his appreciation for Neil Simon still stands…for now. But while reading through his reviews, it seemed to me that John was itching to get behind a camera. So I asked him as much.

"Great question, but no. As a critic, though, I was offered parts in movies, most of which I turned down as a conflict of interest." He paused, then exclaimed, "My god, what an outdated concept that is in America today. But my one regret was not accepting Alan Pakula's offer to play the senator in *The Parallax View.* And another regret I have, a bit off topic, was not saving a love letter from a 73 year-old Josephine Baker following a review I did of her one-woman show."

And now for a commercial break…

Overall, this is a book about movies and John Barbour's reviews of them, but in reading through the stack of articles he'd sent me, I caught the words *Saturday Night Live* in bold and realized that he had reviewed an episode that aired in 1977 and had to share it, especially since it's given me an opportunity to offer my thoughts.

It was about two years earlier when I'd happened upon the comedy sketch show that aired at 11:30 PM every Saturday and found I couldn't stop laughing. Chevy Chase[96] was hysterical and unique, as far as I was concerned, and made it a point to continue watching it every week. But, now, in the year of 2021, it's been ages since I watched it because I don't find it funny and, when I do occasionally manage to catch some of it, I am terribly distracted watching the actors read their lines from cue cards without engaging with each other. It's as if Lorne Michaels[97] doesn't care if the show is phoned in, so to speak, as if there's little to compete with at that hour.

For some reason, I have no memory of the episode that John reviewed. Apparently, after Chevy Chase left to make movies, there was a competition SNL called "Anyone Can Host" and an 80 year-old woman, Miskel Spillman, [98]won. Here's John's take on that event:

The reason the producers of *Saturday Night Live* put together the anyone-can-host contest is that, since the departure of Chevy Chase, it doesn't look as though they know how to put on a *show*. Nowhere was this more pathetically evident than when they aired the one with the winner—an 80-year-old grandmother named Miskel Spillman. From the little they gave her to do in the way of quantity, and with the little they gave her and the competent cast in the way of quality, I don't know if Miskel Spillman ended up thinking she was the winner or the loser.

It was an embarrassment. Evidently the people connected with *Saturday*

Night feel they don't have to be funny, original or clever anymore. They now give the impression that being from New York is enough, that they reside on the Mount Sinai of Satire. Everything on the show is so precious and cutesy these days, it would make the stomach of a real humorist like Robert Benchley[99] turn over in his grave.

Were this show to originate in Los Angeles or Chicago, and if NBC didn't cancel it, the rest of the country would probably cancel L.A. or Chicago. In 90 minutes of the Miskel Spillman show there was only one good line. The rest of the material would have been thrown out the window by a high-school drama class, and the singer, Elvis Costello[100], would have been thrown out by the music class.

Because Miskel Spillman was an 80-year-old grandmother who was closer to the end than the beginning, I was glad she won. That moment on national TV, regardless of its content, will, as that overused song says, light up her life—and the lives of her family and friends. But how thoughtlessly she was used.

With such a woman as host, what a wonderful opportunity there was to do some pointed, funny, meaningful material about what it is like to grow old in America, to comment comically on Social Security, mandatory retirement, loneliness, Lawrence Welk[101], dirty old men, old-age homes, the gray panthers and Lawrence Welk some more. Instead they reduced Spillman to their own juvenile level, implying that before the show she was lying on her back in the dressing room, stoned from smoking pot.

Now that NBC has let Miskel Spillman host the show, they might improve it by letting her produce it. Or better still, hold an anyone-can-produce-and-write-junk-like-this contest.

All I can add to that is, "Amen."

As cheesy the 1933 version of *King Kong* was, it's still my favorite. The one caveat, though, is Fay Wray[102] as Ann Darrow constantly screaming. I also enjoyed watching *Mighty Joe Young*. However, recently it was on TCM and I found myself groaning at some of the dialogue. There's something about massive gorillas that producers believe make entertaining movies and as of this writing there have been twelve Kong movies made, the most recent is *Godzilla vs. Kong*, which was released this year—2021. But in 1976, I suppose there was the thought that with the improvement of special effects, a new version would be so much better. I still prefer the 1933 version, and by the lede, it appears John wasn't a fan of the 1976 version, either.

Giving the Gong to the New 'King Kong'

By John Barbour

A critic trying to review *King Kong* is a little like a dentist trying to warn kids about Coca-Cola; regardless of the cavities, they're going to buy it anyway. And there are cavities in Kong II that even the giant ape could walk through. Still, this Dino De Laurentiis[103] remake will probably take in so much money from kids alone that it will require King Kong to carry it to the bank.

One of the things that made, and still makes, the original *Kong* so effective is that there was always an element of fear and danger present. In this version, there is absolutely none. At times we feel we are not watching a remake so much as a takeoff, *Kong Goes to Camp*. Charles Grodin[104] plays the ambitious head of a geological team who has talked a giant oil conglomerate into letting him explore for oil on a small, mist-shrouded isle in the Pacific. (Grodin's performance incidentally is so broad he looks like he's drilling for *corn* oil.) Then, on the way to the island, they come across Jessica Lange[105], an aspiring starlet, floating on a life raft wearing

a low-cut cocktail dress. She tells her rescuers she owes her life to *Deep Throat*—a producer, she says, was showing it aboard his yacht, and she couldn't look so she went up the deck. That's when the yacht exploded.

What Lange says to humans, however, isn't nearly as dumb as what she says to the ape. On the island, the geological team, which now includes a stowaway Harvard prof (Jeff Bridges[106]), discovers there is no oil. In the meantime, a bunch of natives discover Jessica Lange is now wearing a new halter-top outfit and figure Kong would love it—the girl, not the outfit—so they kidnap her and tie her outside the village. When Kong comes to cart Lange off, she starts screaming at him that he's a "male chauvinist ape," and that, "You're not going to eat me." To prevent this, she starts punching him in the nostrils. And if you think this dialogue is ridiculous, it gets even worse. When the ape settles down a little, Lange tries to calm him further by asking him if he's an Aries.

Jeff Bridges, who is the only believable thing in the film, wants to rescue her. (He's an Aries.) Charles Grodin wants to capture the gorilla—and do you know what for? He thinks it would be great in TV commercials. I can see it now: Mr. Whipple[107], the market man, telling Kong not to squeeze the Charmin, or Mrs. Olson telling him he makes lousy coffee.

This movie was only made to be commercial. In that respect, it will likely succeed. However, if it were not for the first Kong, this one would be *King Gong.*

Notes

1 https://en.wikipedia.org/wiki/Cary_Grant
2 https://en.wikipedia.org/wiki/Clint_Eastwood
3 https://en.wikipedia.org/wiki/President_John_F._Kennedy_Assassination_Records_Collection_Act_of_1992
4 https://en.wikipedia.org/wiki/Upton_Sinclair
5 https://www.rachelcarson.org/
6 https://en.wikipedia.org/wiki/Chicago_Sun-Times
7 https://en.wikipedia.org/wiki/Ron_Howard
8 https://en.wikipedia.org/wiki/Glenn_Ford
9 https://en.wikipedia.org/wiki/Wolfman_Jack
10 https://en.wikipedia.org/wiki/Sandra_Dee
11 https://en.wikipedia.org/wiki/George_Lucas
12 https://en.wikipedia.org/wiki/Diana_Ross
13 https://en.wikipedia.org/wiki/Billie_Holiday
14 https://en.wikipedia.org/wiki/Lana_Turner
15 https://en.wikipedia.org/wiki/Juanita_Moore
16 https://en.wikipedia.org/wiki/Susan_Kohner
17 https://en.wikipedia.org/wiki/John_Gavin
18 https://en.wikipedia.org/wiki/Walter_Cronkite
19 https://en.wikipedia.org/wiki/Mahalia_Jackson
20 https://barackobama.com/
21 https://en.wikipedia.org/wiki/Billy_Dee_Williams
22 https://en.wikipedia.org/wiki/Sidney_J._Furie
23 https://de.m.wikipedia.org/wiki/Terence_McCloy
24 https://en.wikipedia.org/wiki/Chris_Clark_(singer)
25 https://en.wikipedia.org/wiki/Suzanne_de_Passe
26 https://en.wikipedia.org/wiki/Ku_Klux_Klan
27 https://en.wikipedia.org/wiki/Burt_Bacharach
28 https://en.wikipedia.org/wiki/The_Beatles
29 https://en.wikipedia.org/wiki/Michel_Legrand
30 https://en.wikipedia.org/wiki/Richard_Pryor
31 https://en.wikipedia.org/wiki/Andra_Day
32 https://en.wikipedia.org/wiki/Bradley_Cooper
33 https://en.wikipedia.org/wiki/Lady_Gaga
34 https://en.wikipedia.org/wiki/Judy_Garland
35 https://en.wikipedia.org/wiki/James_Mason
36 https://en.wikipedia.org/wiki/Janet_Gaynor

37 https://en.wikipedia.org/wiki/Fredric_March
38 https://en.wikipedia.org/wiki/Barbra_Streisand
39 https://en.wikipedia.org/wiki/Harpo_Marx
40 https://www.dictionary.com/browse/lp long playing; long play: 1.a vinyl phonograph record played at 33 1/3 rpm and typically containing seven or more tracks, or one or more long classical pieces.
41 https://en.wikipedia.org/wiki/Fred_Allen
42 https://en.wikipedia.org/wiki/Corrie_ten_Boom
43 https://en.wikipedia.org/wiki/Jeannette_Clift_George
44 https://en.wikipedia.org/wiki/Julie_Harris
45 This was in reference to the other movie, Dog Day Afternoon, that John was reviewing in the same issue
46 https://en.wikipedia.org/wiki/Eileen_Heckart
47 https://en.wikipedia.org/wiki/Arthur_O%27Connell
48 https://en.wikipedia.org/wiki/Norman_Jewison
49 https://en.wikipedia.org/wiki/Melinda_Dillon
50 https://en.wikipedia.org/wiki/Teri_Garr
51 https://en.wikipedia.org/wiki/Bob_Balaban
52 https://en.wikipedia.org/wiki/Paine_Webber
53 https://en.wikipedia.org/wiki/Julia_Phillips
54 https://en.wikipedia.org/wiki/Michael_Phillips_(producer)
55 https://en.wikipedia.org/wiki/Tinkertoy
56 https://en.wikipedia.org/wiki/Bermuda_Triangle
57 https://en.wikipedia.org/wiki/Douglas_Trumbull
58 https://en.wikipedia.org/wiki/John_Williams
59 https://en.wikipedia.org/wiki/Vilmos_Zsigmond
60 https://en.wikipedia.org/wiki/Watergate_scandal
61 https://en.wikipedia.org/wiki/Carl_Bernstein
62 https://en.wikipedia.org/wiki/Bob_Woodward
63 https://en.wikipedia.org/wiki/William_Goldman
64 https://en.wikipedia.org/wiki/Ben_Bradlee
65 https://en.wikipedia.org/wiki/Hal_Holbrook
66 https://en.wikipedia.org/wiki/Margaux_Hemingway
67 https://en.wikipedia.org/wiki/Mariel_Hemingway
68 https://en.wikipedia.org/wiki/Ernest_Hemingway
69 https://en.wikipedia.org/wiki/Charles_Bronson
70 https://en.wikipedia.org/wiki/Chris_Sarandon
71 https://www.nytimes.com/2021/05/19/arts/aaron-stern-dead.html
72 https://en.wikipedia.org/wiki/John_Travolta

73 https://en.wikipedia.org/wiki/Bee_Gees
74 https://en.wikipedia.org/wiki/Jennifer_Beals
75 https://en.wikipedia.org/wiki/Kevin_Bacon
76 https://en.wikipedia.org/wiki/Steve_Edwards_(talk_show_host)
77 https://worldradiohistory.com/hd2/IDX-Business/Magazines/Broadcasting-IDX/1977-Broadcasting/1977-02-14-Broadcasting-Page-0121.pdf
78 https://en.wikipedia.org/wiki/Richard_M._Daley
79 https://en.wikipedia.org/wiki/Charles_MacArthur
80 https://en.wikipedia.org/wiki/Jim_Murray_(sportswriter)
81 https://en.wikipedia.org/wiki/Paul_Conrad
82 https://en.wikipedia.org/wiki/John_Leonard_(critic)
83 https://en.wikipedia.org/wiki/Mike_Royko
84 https://en.wikipedia.org/wiki/Clarence_Darrow
85 https://en.wikipedia.org/wiki/Anita_Bryant
86 https://en.wikipedia.org/wiki/Carl_Sandburg
87 https://en.wikipedia.org/wiki/Fred_Astaire
88 https://en.wikipedia.org/wiki/David_Berkowitz
89 https://en.wikipedia.org/wiki/Albert_Schweitzer
90 https://en.wikipedia.org/wiki/Regis_Philbin
91 https://en.wikipedia.org/wiki/Farrah_Fawcett
92 https://en.wikipedia.org/wiki/Thomas_Noguchi
93 https://en.wikipedia.org/wiki/Olivia_Newton-John
94 https://en.wikipedia.org/wiki/Quinn_Cummings
95 https://en.wikipedia.org/wiki/Marsha_Mason
96 https://en.wikipedia.org/wiki/Chevy_Chase
97 https://en.wikipedia.org/wiki/Lorne_Michaels
98 https://en.wikipedia.org/wiki/Miskel_Spillman
99 https://en.wikipedia.org/wiki/Robert_Benchley
100 https://en.wikipedia.org/wiki/Elvis_Costello
101 https://en.wikipedia.org/wiki/Lawrence_Welk
102 https://en.wikipedia.org/wiki/Fay_Wray
103 https://en.wikipedia.org/wiki/Dino_De_Laurentiis
104 https://en.wikipedia.org/wiki/Charles_Grodin
105 https://en.wikipedia.org/wiki/Jessica_Lange
106 https://en.wikipedia.org/wiki/Jeff_Bridges
107 https://en.wikipedia.org/wiki/Mr._Whipple

V. Movies I Didn't See...But Wish I Had

There are just some movies that it's assumed, at least by me, that everyone has seen and loved. Yet, here I am confessing that I somehow missed out on some that I should have seen by now. However, that doesn't mean I won't, especially after reading John's reviews of the ones he liked or at least appreciated, which I'll share in this chapter. So let's begin.

I've always enjoyed Paul Newman[1] and Robert Redford, but was never interested in watching *The Sting*, which came out in 1973. It didn't show up quietly. No, it was a phenomenal success and went on to being nominated for ten Oscars. It won seven, including Best Picture, Best Director, Best Film Editing, and Best Writing for original screenplay. Redford was nominated for Best Actor but Jack Lemmon[2] won for *Save the Tiger*, another movie I haven't seen. Even with all those awards, I never made it a point to watch *The Sting* when it came on TV. But that may change. Here's why:

On the Con with the Doublemint Twins

By John Barbour

It's hard to believe two guys who are down and out could have such good teeth...

There is not much bite to *The Sting*, but it does have some pleasant touches. Two of them are the doublemint twins[3], Robert Redford and Paul Newman. Redford is a smalltime con man during the Depression, a condition which he feels is permanent in his life; he has no desire to make anything more than a five or ten dollar hit on the streets, which he shares with his partners, a wispy white and an old, seasoned black. By accident, though, they rip off a bagman with the mob, and by intent the head of the mob. Robert Shaw has part of the black's body ripped off then sends his guns out after Redford.

Redford's ambition now is elevated to getting even. He says he hasn't had the practice to kill Shaw, but he does have the guts to con him. To help him learn how to pull that off he goes to Chicago to talk to Paul Newman, the last of the Great Con Artists. He finds Paul in a drunken stupor in a whore house…probably trying to forget *Pocket Money* and *Judge Roy Bean*. They team up, and while they go about winning Shaw's money, Redford is trying to avoid losing his life.

David Ward[4] has written a script that's as well plotted as the heist, and although a lot of the interaction between the characters is predictable, director George Roy Hill[5] keeps the story skipping along on the surface so that it doesn't sink long enough for the audience to ask questions.

There is a kind of easy charm and style in the overall production which is hindered a bit by some brief violence. You overlook that, though. You also overlook Shaw's English accent as the head of the New York Irish Mafia because the rest of his performance is so perfect.

As for Redford and Newman, their presence makes the film a little more interesting and fun to watch. You are not quite sure if they're conning Shaw or the audience. It's just a little too difficult to believe that those two guys could be down and out and have such good teeth.

As it happens, in the same issue following the review for *The Sting*, was another review for a movie that I am loathe to admit I haven't yet seen. So let's get right to the review:

Serpico should have been retitled *Pacino*. His performance is more interesting than the film. You know he has to be good because only once or twice do you ever stop to think how much he looks like Dustin Hoffman.

Serpico tells the story of a young Italian-American son of a bookmaker who wanted to be an honest New York cop in the worst way, and discovered that to be an honest New York cop was the worst way. As a law abiding rookie he found he was as welcome among New York's Finest as Ralph Nader[6] was at General Motors. Serpico was the officer who blew the whistle on police payoffs before a New York grand jury. This led to the establishment of the Knapp Commission[7] which investigated and uncovered the incredible corruption in that city's police department.

What with all the bigtime corruption we have been hearing about in government and corporations, the timing of this movie couldn't have been better, but its execution could have been. It doesn't quite come off as drama or as documentary. The settings are real—the greasy police stations and the dirty streets—but we don't feel as though we're there; we see the massive corruption but we don't feel any indignation. We see Serpico surrounded by cops who hate him, but we don't feel any of his aloneness or frustration, and when he is set up by fellow officers to be shot in the face by a junkie, we don't feel any terror.

There is no sense of loss and there is no sense of victory. A true story has been turned into a movie that lacks true drama or tension; as a result we become observers instead of participants, and what we are observing mostly is not Serpico the good cop, but Pacino the brilliant actor. Not only does he carry the film, he carries the audience. To show you how interesting it is watching him perform, when he and his first girlfriend in the film (a lovely dancer) are sitting nude facing one another in a bathtub and she tells him about a Texan she is interested in, you'll find yourself not looking at her breasts, but at Pacino's eyes...and not just because they're bigger.

Even though I never saw *Serpico*, I was familiar with the story, and deeply disturbed by it. I tend to get frustrated by those who wield power and threats to hide their own illegal activities, so watching the story unfold would only infuriate me. Still, because it is Al Pacino in the lead role, one that earned him a Golden Globe for Best Actor, I'm thinking it would be well worth watching this movie.

There are some movies where I've seen snippets or bigger portions, but not the entire film. One of those would be *One Flew over the Cuckoo's Nest* (1975). (Did I just hear a groan?) I know, it's a classic but I somehow didn't make it a point of watching it. According to Wikipedia, it was considered to be one of the best films ever made, having won all five major Academy Award categories: Best picture, Actor in a leading role, Actress in a leading role, Director and Screenplay. That's impressive. I wonder if John was as head over heels about this flick as those who hand out Oscars were:

At the end of *One Flew over the Cuckoo's Nest*, you feel as if you have just watched a good game in which the Los Angeles Rams played to a tie. You liked it, but there is that slightly frustrating feeling that there was one missing element which could have made it a real winner. That is the paradox of director Milos Forman's[8] otherwise fascinating film in which there are some magnificent performances—especially that of Jack Nicholson, whose screen presence could get him an automatic first down with almost any woman in the audience. Nicholson portrays an incorrigible convict with three months to serve who is sent to a mental hospital for psychiatric evaluation. His therapy group consists of nine patients—some there voluntarily, some not, but all with minds as distorted as their faces.

Their nurse is an emotionless bureaucrat whose fixation with routine perpetuates the system more than it promotes cures. Nicholson thinks the "crazies" (as he calls them) are as normal as anybody walking the street, and that it's the system that's goofy; so to prove this, using a bit of 'creative nonconformity" he gets his nutty nine involved in such weird escapades as passing themselves off as doctors, chartering a fishing boat and getting a painfully shy, stammering man his first woman.

However, because of the inevitable conflict with the system, the joy of these moments soon dissolves into tragedy. Only when the system inflicts its final penalty, and there is no feeling of outrage, do you realize what's missing: feeling. It's not just the nurse who's emotionless, but much of the movie. Because the film only shows the results of bizarre behavior without really getting us to feel moved by it, *One Flew over the Cuckoo's Nest*, although excellent in many respects, still leaves us interested spectators rather than involved participants.

Okay, so it seems as though John wasn't as crazy about this movie as other critics were, but still he'd said enough to make me watch it the next time it airs.

As an aside, Netflix wanted viewers of *One Flew over the Cuckoo's Nest* to understand why the nurse was emotionless and made the movie titled *Ratched*, as in Nurse Ratched, starring Sarah Paulson[9]. My daughter insisted that I give the movie a try. I did, but didn't stick with it. Instead, I watched *Grace and Frankie* for the umpteenth time. It was during the pandemic and I needed to laugh. Maybe, though, after I finally watch *One Flew over the Cuckoo's Nest*, I'll give *Ratched* a chance. *Maybe*.

Here's the thing: I can't recall if I've seen some of the movies that John reviewed since the plot seems familiar to me but I have no clear memory of having seen said movie. This is the case with *Dog Day Afternoon*. I may have seen portions of it or just read enough about it to be familiar with it. So, I'm going to assume that I hadn't seen this one and read what John thought of it.

Pacino's 'Dog Day' Has Both Bark and Bite

By John Barbour

John Wayne[10] became a superstar without ever having to leave the West; Al Pacino is going to become a superstar without ever leaving New York City. From the incorruptible cop in *Serpico*, to the son in *The Godfather*, and now to the bizarrely bigamous bank robber in a fabulous film called *Dog Day Afternoon*, Pacino demonstrates that of the 8 million stories—as *Naked City* used to say—in that city, Pacino has the talent to do all of them.

Dog Day Afternoon is based on a real incident: two armed men were trapped by law enforcement officers while attempting to hold up a Brooklyn bank a few years ago, one of the men (the one played by Pacino) a bisexual. In exchange for a jet that would fly them to freedom, the robbers offered to free the employees who were being held hostage. From the very opening scenes of the film, director Sidney Lumet[11] and writer Frank Pierson[12] establish brilliantly the mood of the movie and the character of Pacino: early in the holdup, when Pacino finally gets the nerve to pull his rifle out of its flower-box-disguised case, he can't shake the box's ribbon off the gun; when he and his buddy—played perfectly by John Cazale[13]—get to the vault, they find out the money has just been picked up by the Brink's truck and only $1,500 is left; and Pacino can't quite bring himself to lock the girls in the vault because one of them has to go to the bathroom.

You almost have the feeling you're watching a comedy, but the underlying intensity is such that you know at any moment the mirth could tumble into tragedy and madness. When the trapped Pacino asks to see his wife—and the "wife" turns out to be a male mental patient whose sex-change operation Pacino has set the robbery up to finance—you don't know whether to laugh or cry; and it's the same dilemma when he talks to his *other* wife, an exceedingly nagging woman who could be Shamu's[14] understudy. The mood gets even darker and even more nervously funny when the TV cameras turn Pacino, like Patty Hearst[15], into a News Event Superstar, with the spectators as audience and the hostages—and even a delivery boy—as walk-on celebrities...while all the time the cops are setting up for the kill.

Dog Day Afternoon is a superior film. Its profound insights hurt only when you laugh, and you laugh a lot.

That settles it. I must make it a point to watch *Dog Day Afternoon.* As an aside, sadly John Cazale died of lung cancer in 1978, three years after *Dog Day Afternoon* came out. At his side was Meryl Streep who lived with him for those three years and who is quoted saying: "I didn't get over it. I don't want to get over it. No matter what you do, the pain is always there in some recess of your mind, and it affects everything that happens afterwards. I think you can assimilate the pain and go on without making an obsession of it."

Quite likely, I won't be able to watch the movie without thinking about this sad, real-life ending.

In 1975, *The Day of the Locust* was brought to the big screen, but I missed it much to my chagrin. Here's why:

Hollywood: Through a Microscope Darkly

By John Barbour

Failures, junkies and a few good reasons to be wary of reincarnation

I think audiences will feel the same way about *The Day of the Locust* as they do about Tom Snyder's[16] style as a newscaster or talk-show host: they will either love it or hate it, but they will watch it.

In this film adaptation, director John Schlesinger[17] (*Midnight Cowboy*) is visually faithful to the Nathanael West[18] novel, which focuses on an assortment of intriguingly bizarre characters on the fringes of failure in Hollywood during the mid-'30s. He uses his camera like a microscope, peering in large close ups at the people who are infected with the germ of failure and self-deception, and this accounts for the successful and compelling look of the film. But it is also responsible for the failings. There is virtually no character with whom you can empathize—you don't mind looking down the microscope, but you don't want to get too close for fear of contamination.

The cast, however, is excellent—Karen Black[19] as a movie extra who talks of stardom but remains a loser, walking through life and her relationships as though some hidden camera were filming her; Donald Sutherland[20], as the emotionally paralyzed accountant who'll subsidize her without sleeping with her; and William Atherton, as the aspiring studio artist whose fascination for these misfits causes him to paint his own life into a corner. And there are two other fine performances: Burgess Meredith[21] as Karen's father, a failed vaudevillian-turned-salesman who now dances door to door, and Billy Barty[22] as a lascivious showbiz dwarf.

The movie is supposed to build to a closing scene where the deliberate killing of a child at a movie premiere goads the once-cheering crowd into an orgy of death and destruction—like a plague of locusts. But, also like the locust, this scene comes out of nowhere; to the viewer, it appears unmotivated and unrelated to the rest of the film. In a sense, one's reaction to this climax epitomizes Schlesinger's failure throughout the film: like all riots, it's interesting to watch, but you don't want to get involved.

John is right: that is an impressive cast. One of my favorites, though, is Burgess Meredith. Readers may remember him from *Rocky* as Rocky's trainer but I'll always and forever remember him in the *Twilight Zone* and the episode titled "Time Enough At Last" where he was obsessed with books and all he wanted to do was read. Oh, the irony of how that episode ends and his pitiful voice as he says, "That's not fair. That's not fair at all. There was time now. There was, was all the time I needed..."

Now I look forward to seeing him in *The Day of the Locust.*

Even though I saw only one or two of the movies that were nominated each year for an Oscar, I would eagerly anticipate watching the Academy

Awards. I found it to be great entertainment. (Later, in the book, we'll find out what John thinks about the Oscars.) So, in 1978, after I put my baby boy to bed, I watched the 50th Academy Awards, hosted by Bob Hope. Quite likely, I knew something about *I Never Promised You a Rose Garden*, nominated for best screenplay, and based on the novel with the same name. (I may have even read that novel.) But I somehow missed the movie. I suppose as a new mother, I missed a lot of movies, and was fine with it. But thanks to John, I now find out just what I missed with what had to have been a disturbing albeit intriguing film.

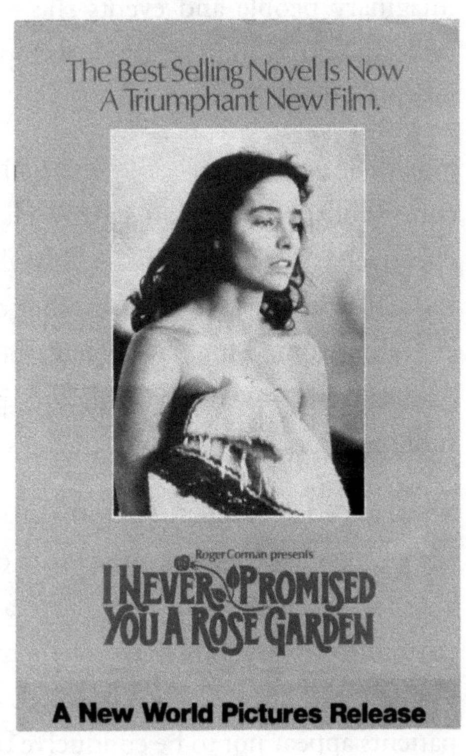

The Best Selling Novel Is Now
A Triumphant New Film.
Roger Corman presents
I NEVER PROMISED
YOU A ROSE GARDEN
A New World Pictures Release

I Never Promised You a Rose Garden is a painful film to watch. It's the story of an intensely disturbed and suicidal 16-year-old schizophrenic girl who is committed to a psychiatric hospital. The commitment of director Anthony Page[23] and writers Gavin Lambert[24] and Lewis John Carlino[25] to treating the subject with sincerity and compassion—and the scope and depth of the performances, especially Kathleen Quinlan's[26] as the girl—overcomes many of the film's flaws and keeps the audience in their seats even though the anguish in some scenes may make them turn their heads from the screen.

The girl is brought to the hospital by her parents, and she is such a schizoid that not only does she retreat into her own weird world—peopled by bizarre natives and lepers—but in order to function in it she also invents her own language. She is so numbed and poisoned by self-loathing that she can't feel it when she slashes her wrists, cuts open her arm with a tin can, or burns holes in her skin with cigarette butts. But *we* can. Yet we are not made to feel and understand the real roots of her illness. We hear her tell her psychiatrist—played with magnificent restraint by Bibi Andersson[27]—that her parents sent her to some surgeons who she claimed butchered her in removing a vaginal tumor; we also hear her tell Bibi about early sexual repressions and an attempt to murder her younger sister. But instead of showing us how the girl sees these actual incidents through a mind that was misshaped by them, we see only the imaginary people and events she sees. As a result, we lose a sense of understanding, and the film loses a potential for an even greater sense of terror and drama.

What continues to give the film its impact and focus is the passion and control of Quinlan as an actress. Had the visuals been structured more effectively, the moment in the film when, after three years in the hospital, the girl sears her skin with another cigarette and shrieks with *happiness* at feeling something would have been much more profound. Instead of just being moved by Quinlan's performance, we would have been sublimely touched by the character's ecstasy and self-discovery.

There are other excellent performances, but the humor that emerges from the women patients is not the black comedy of *Cuckoo's Nest*. It is deeper and darker. Aside from that, there are two interesting impressions that emerge from the film—one of them intentional, the other accidental. The first is that psychiatric hospitals themselves, the staffs and the other patients appear not to be conducive to curing mental illness; in fact, they may compound and complicate treatment. The other is that, watching the patients, one gets the feeling that mental illness is almost voluntary—that there is no such thing as mental disorder, only aberrant behavior, which a person chooses to indulge in because acting insane is easier than coping with the disciplines of being sane.

I Never Promised You a Rose Garden ends up a rose bush. There are some thorns, but there are also some moments that blossom.

What a heavy movie and yet one that I would want to see, but I think switching gears to something lighter makes sense. The year is 1978. The movie? *Same Time, Next Year.*

Alan Alda and Ellen Burstyn

A Hawkeye Is a Hawkeye, but a Burstyn...

By John Barbour

In the manner of Neil Simon, who is a genius of this genre, author Bernard Slade[28] has written the perfect two-character comedy in *Same Time, Next Year*, one that will be playing in stock somewhere every year. It is an entertaining American four-poster which shows that two married people can stay together for more than 25 years by not being married to each other.

In translating his own play to the screen, Slade suffers less than Simon from the claustrophobia inherent in adapting a one set theater piece to a large screen. Simon's characters in his best plays are mostly New York Jewish; on screen he is able to retain their caustic, cutting wit but seems to almost deny their identity, making the characters somehow amorphous. Slade's wit is softer, but so are his people. This softness gives the characters a dimension that often overcomes the confines of the setting.

One of Slade's people in this polished Robert Mulligan[29] production is an accountant, George (played by Alan Alda[30]), who makes a sentimental journey every year from New Jersey to California to do the books of his first client. While staying at an inn the first year he meets Doris (Ellen Burstyn), an Irish-American high-school dropout and mother of three who is beating a retreat to a Catholic retreat to avoid the family's yearly visit to her mother-in-law in Bakersfield.

George and Doris get involved in their first affair, and it's so fantastic that in spite of the guilt, most of which is George's, they decide to meet once a year from then on. They begin in 1951 and meet every year—through the McCarthy era, the Bay of Pigs invasion, assassinations, the Vietnam War, heart attacks and the tooth fairy—up until 1977, making love 110 times. (As an accountant, George just can't stop tabulating on his new calculator.)

The film picks them up every five years; the bridges to these scenes are arresting black-and-white photo montages, compiled by Chuck Braverman[31] and Ken Rudolph[32] that depict the personalities, events and fads that dominated the era. And these montages add a greater sense of honesty and reality to a plot that at times touches on R-rated sitcom, albeit good sitcom.

In addition, both performers are excellent. On screen, Alda has the likable quality of a Jack Lemmon on Valium; however, even though his character over the years goes from an uptight accountant to a gestalt piano player, he only seems to change clothes, never personality. Burstyn, on the other hand, whose character goes from high-school dropout to Book-of-the Month Club member to antiwar protestor to successful businesswoman, would never have had to change costumes; with each transition she is achingly believable and comically touching.

Finally, of course, there is Slade, who has written some dynamite dialogue. The straightforward sincerity of his approach to the characters is probably what has gotten this fine film a PG rating, whereas in any other hands it would have gotten an R. The primary attraction between Doris and George is sex; for 25 years of their lives and one hour of the film all they talk about is George's erection or lack of it and his guilt or lack of it over his erection or lack of it. Perhaps the rating board figured it was suitable for children because if there weren't any erections, there wouldn't be any kids.

There's so much about what John wrote in his review that makes me want to somehow find a way to watch this movie, sooner rather than later. First, I love the idea of being able to witness history happening within this storyline. Writers who pay attention to what is happening in the real world and incorporate it in the fictional world get high marks from me and, apparently, from John as well.

Here's one that came out in 1976; I have no memory of ever hearing about it but after reading John's review, I would love to see if I could somehow come across it. Even though I was never a fan of Shelley Winters, (something about her put me off) it seems like it would be a great movie to watch on a chilly Sunday afternoon. Let's see if you agree.

Shelley's Long and Whining Road Finally Pays Off

By John Barbour

Love, dreams and Momism in 'Greenwich Village'

If they gave Oscars for whining, Shelley Winters would have a roomful of them—beginning with *A Place in the Sun*, in which she kept bugging Montgomery Clift[33] to marry her. She so bugs *me* as an actress that when I think back on that scene where Clift finally drowns her, I never think of him as an actor but as a critic.

Because of my aversion to her and her kinds of characters, I never thought I could like her in a film until I saw *Next Stop, Greenwich Village*—and loved her. There is no question that, come next year, she will be a strong Oscar contender for her magnificently heavyweight performance as an oversized Jewish mother. She is so perfect as Mrs. Lapinsky (a sort of mean, meddlesome Molly Goldberg[34]) in this excellent Paul Mazursky[35] film that it seems like her whole career was preparation for the part. Like Brando in *The Godfather*, even when she's not on the screen you feel her presence.

Every Jewish mother, of course, has to have a son; and, in this film, Winters' is played by Lenny Baker[36], who looks a little like a Jewish Jimmie Walker[37]—and who turns in a performance that is also dyn-o-mite! In fact, from the opening scene, you know you are going to see a very special film—one that is funny, one that is sad—because it is so real. The son, Larry, is packing to move to Greenwich Village to become an actor, and his mother is crushed. She loves him so much that when he tries to kiss her goodbye, she punches him.

When Larry moves, his new apartment is barren, but his life is full of wonderfully human characters and, although set in the '50s, they and their dreams are ageless: the young German who wants to be a hyphenate…a writer-lover; a pathetic, orphaned black homosexual who wants to be either Jewish or loved; a joyless woman who practices suicide till practice makes perfect; and Lenny's faithless girlfriend, who dreams of Mexico and a diaphragm.

And if you've dreamed lately of seeing an honest, worthwhile movie, your next stop should be *Next Stop, Greenwich Village.*

As it happens, Winters wasn't nominated for an Oscar for this movie, but after my research I am even more determined to find this movie since I discovered that this was Bill Murray's[38] first movie, even though he wasn't credited, and also Jeff Goldblum[39] and Christopher Walken had roles in it.

I love it when a comedy movie can keep me laughing, especially when it makes me feel as though I am in on the joke, which is why I thoroughly enjoy Mel Brooks.[40] Yet, for some reason, I missed *Silent Movie* (1976). Perhaps again, it could be because I was a young mother caring for my son and getting out anywhere was a challenge. Thankfully, reading John's reviews is a great reminder to try and catch it at some point. Here's John's review of *Silent Movie*:

Mel Brooks and Woody Allen are cult comics. To me, though, most of their movies consist only of a half-dozen good jokes, a couple of good sight gags and an hour of excess celluloid. In Brooks' *Blazing Saddles*, the one terrific moment that made you almost forget how tacky the rest of the film was occurred when Alex Karras[41] punched out a horse. Can you imagine what a fabulously funny film you would have if most of it consisted of this kind of deliciously inventive sight gag?

Well, that film is *Silent Movie*. Brooks should either throw away his typewriter or give it to Neil Simon, because with this film, based on an idea by Ron Clark[42] and co-authored by Rudy De Luca[43] and Barry Levinson[44], Brooks has made not only the funniest American film in five years but, visually, the most creatively funny film since *Mr. Hulot's Holiday*. The only word in it is spoken by Marcel Marceau[45], and it's a good thing there's no other dialogue because you probably wouldn't hear it for the laughs.

Just like in the old silent movies, printed cards pop up occasionally to advance the plot and let us know what the characters are supposed to be saying—even though sometimes their lips are moving differently.

Its setting is Hollywood, and Brooks plays a former film director and a former lush. Along with his sidekicks, played by Dom Deluise and Marty Feldman[46], the cards tell us he's trying to talk to a studio chief (Sid Caesar) into letting him make a silent movie.

Caesar agrees, but only on the condition that the project include some big stars. So Brooks and his Dynamically Dumb Duo set out to sign Burt Reynolds, James Caan, Liza Minelli[47] and Paul Newman. The result is a sequence of sometimes inspired sight gags indicating that Reynolds and the other biggies had more fun doing cameos in this movie than starring in vehicles of their own.

Although rated PG, *Silent Movie* could really be a G; unlike a couple of Brooks' other films, there's nothing in this that's either tacky or tasteless. Although the obligatory Brooks' Anal Joke is present, it's merely funny: while he and Bernadette Peters[48] are riding a carousel, their painted pony stops and defecates wooden alphabet blocks.

Brooks has proven silence can be golden—and a joy. This is one picture that's worth a thousand laughs.

Oh my goodness, while copying his review for this book, I couldn't stop laughing at the very idea of this movie. I had no idea that it had such a stellar cast. As of this writing, Mel Brooks is 95 years old. Sadly, the sidekicks he's worked with, including Sid Caesar[49] and Carl Reiner[50], have all passed but their genius lives on thanks to their movies.

The next movie I'd missed and wish I hadn't hit the theaters in 1977: *Looking for Mr. Goodbar*. First, in looking up information about this movie, I was surprised that Richard Gere[51] was in it. If I'd known that back in 1977, I might have made a point to go see it and drool. Second, I didn't realize the soundtrack had hits that included *Don't Leave Me This Way, Love Hangover* and *Back Stabbers.* Not too far from where I live there's a record store that sells vintage albums and CDs and I may have to see if they have the soundtrack to this movie, a movie I need to watch.

No, I'm Oscar, But I'll Go Home with You

By John Barbour

Goodbar was just looking for Keaton

Not just anyone could have made *Looking for Mr. Goodbar* into a movie—and not just anyone should see it. In translating to the screen Judith Rossner's[52] best-selling tale of a young teacher who prowls around New York singles bars looking for sex, director-writer Richard Brooks[53] has created his best, most meaningful work. It is an uncompromisingly honest and sublimely disciplined and inspired piece of filmmaking.

Diane Keaton—as a woman to whom one man is too many and a million not enough—would probably have to go through a thousand scripts and two careers before hitting on a character as demanding, human and totally fascinating as Theresa Dunn. And Richard Brooks could never have found another actress to perform it so perfectly.

Theresa is the daughter of unloving, God-fearing Irish Catholics: her father (Richard Kiley[54]) pushed morality so far down her throat that she threw up immorality. As a girl, her body lay for a year in a cast, motionless, while her parents told her it was God's will. When she got older, she let almost any man use her body for a night at *his* will. The nude scenes are very explicit and daring, but Brooks handles the story with such insight and care that the more his camera shows Theresa's body, the more we see of her psyche and soul. Thus our affection for her grows, as does our fear for her well-being—a woman who will pick up any man will soon pick up the wrong one. Eventually, of course, she does.

Brilliantly and imperceptibly throughout the film, Brooks plants the dramatic seeds of impending and irreversible horror—seeds that are really the outgrowth of Theresa's own personality and behavior. And the sense of terror grows with the knowledge that every guy she brings home—from the social worker to the Vietnam veteran—is increasingly more capable of rags and cruelty. After one weirdo punches her in the face, her sister (Tuesday Weld[55]) rushes into her filthy apartment to help her. When Weld places a kitchen towel to Keaton's swollen lips, cockroaches fall out onto her chest—an incredible scene! To further add to the tone of the film, while the sister has abortions and orgies, marries and divorces a Jew, in the eyes of their father she does nothing wrong. Keaton, however, who remains single and practices birth control, can do nothing right. This contrast adds a dimension of true tragedy to her fate, which is made to seem as unfair as it is inevitable. Indeed. *Looking for Mr. Goodbar* is a masterpiece of compelling contrasts: It is beautiful and it is base, and the ending is brutal but bearable.

Diane Keaton will unquestionably get an Oscar nomination, and at Academy Award time there might be two of them waiting for Mr. Brooks.

Unfortunately, Keaton and Brooks didn't earn a nomination, but Tuesday Weld did for Best Supporting Actress and William Fraker[56] for Best Cinematography. Either way, I am sold and eager for the opportunity to see this one.

As a young child, probably too young to be watching the TV series *Dr. Kildare*, but even though I was so young, I appreciated the good looking actor who played Dr. Kildare: Richard Chamberlain[57]. I had no idea at the time that he was gay, and in the words of Seinfeld and his friends, "Not that there's anything wrong with that." So in 1973 when *The Three Musketeers* was released with Richard Chamberlain in the cast it's odd that I didn't want to see it, but I suppose the topic didn't intrigue me enough. Now, after reading John's review, that was a mistake on my part.

Getting It Right Once and for All (and All for One)

By John Barbour

There'll be no need to make another "Three Musketeers" now that Richard Lester's version is here...

Hollywood has a tendency to remake old movies. Fred Allen once described Hollywood producers as termites who are constantly chewing on their own backlog. Maybe their idea is to keep redoing certain films until they get them right.

The latest film to be remade is *The Three Musketeers* and I guarantee you it will never be remade again; this time they finally got it right. With this most recent version of Alexandre Dumas[58] classic, director Richard Lester[59] has created his own classic. It is one of the most entertaining, imaginative, and altogether fun movies you will ever see.

The intellectuals in the house will absolutely revel in the deliciously offbeat satire and sight-gags. Lester and writer George Fraser[60] have executed these moments with an underplayed comic consistency that borders on genius. Kids will love the action and the spectacle.

Filmed on location in Spain *Musketeer's* production values are so lush the film looks like it cost more than the country's worth. There's one stunning scene, on the screen only a minute or so, that will give you some idea of the kind of thought and expense that went into the production. It's meant to show us how exquisitely bored the king is: on the front lawn of one of Spain's colossal palaces, in an area the size of half a basketball court, there is a huge black and white chess board. The chessmen are real dogs, cats, and their trainers. From the palace porch a hundred yards away, the king relays via couriers instructions for the next move. At the end of the game there's a fight when a German shepherd looks like he's going to checkmate a French poodle.

The cast includes a dozen internationally known stars, among them Faye Dunaway, Michael York[61], Oliver Reed,[62] Richard Chamberlain, Charlton Heston, and Raquel Welch[63]. Everything about *The Three Musketeers* is so outstanding you'll not only forget there was ever an earlier version, you may even forget that Heston was ever Moses or that Raquel was the *Kansas City Bomber*.

Well, as it happens, there were some more versions made after the 1973 version:

The Three Musketeers (1993), a 1993 Disney adaptation starring Charlie Sheen[64], Kiefer Sutherland[65], Oliver Platt[66] and Chris O'Donnell[67].

The Musketeer, a 2001 film.

The Three Musketeers (2011), directed by Paul W. S. Anderson[68] and starring Luke Evans[69], Ray Stevenson[70] and Milla Jovovich[71].

I didn't see any of those either, but will certainly look for the 1973 version. However, I did follow up with John to see if he stayed true to his word from when he wrote the above review and he replied, "Never saw them. I never thought the version I saw could be improved upon!" So, he never changed his mind! That's John Barbour for you!

Notes

1 https://en.wikipedia.org/wiki/Paul_Newman
2 https://en.wikipedia.org/wiki/Jack_Lemmon
3 https://en.wikipedia.org/wiki/Doublemint
4 https://en.wikipedia.org/wiki/David_S._Ward
5 https://en.wikipedia.org/wiki/George_Roy_Hill
6 https://en.wikipedia.org/wiki/Ralph_Nader
7 https://en.wikipedia.org/wiki/Knapp_Commission
8 https://en.wikipedia.org/wiki/Milo%C5%A1_Forman
9 https://en.wikipedia.org/wiki/Sarah_Paulson
10 https://en.wikipedia.org/wiki/John_Wayne
11 https://en.wikipedia.org/wiki/Sidney_Lumet
12 https://en.wikipedia.org/wiki/Frank_Pierson
13 https://en.wikipedia.org/wiki/John_Cazale
14 https://en.wikipedia.org/wiki/Shamu_(SeaWorld_show)
15 https://en.wikipedia.org/wiki/Patty_Hearst
16 https://en.wikipedia.org/wiki/Tom_Snyder
17 https://en.wikipedia.org/wiki/John_Schlesinger
18 https://en.wikipedia.org/wiki/Nathanael_West
19 https://en.wikipedia.org/wiki/Karen_Black
20 https://en.wikipedia.org/wiki/Donald_Sutherland
21 https://en.wikipedia.org/wiki/Burgess_Meredith
22 https://en.wikipedia.org/wiki/Billy_Barty
23 https://en.wikipedia.org/wiki/Anthony_Page
24 https://en.wikipedia.org/wiki/Gavin_Lambert
25 https://en.wikipedia.org/wiki/Lewis_John_Carlino
26 https://en.wikipedia.org/wiki/Kathleen_Quinlan
27 https://en.wikipedia.org/wiki/Bibi_Andersson
28 https://en.wikipedia.org/wiki/Bernard_Slade
29 https://en.wikipedia.org/wiki/Robert_Mulligan
30 https://en.wikipedia.org/wiki/Alan_Alda
31 https://en.wikipedia.org/wiki/Charles_Braverman
32 http://www.afana.org/rudolphken.htm
33 https://en.wikipedia.org/wiki/Montgomery_Clift
34 https://en.wikipedia.org/wiki/Gertrude_Berg
35 https://en.wikipedia.org/wiki/Paul_Mazursky
36 https://en.wikipedia.org/wiki/Lenny_Baker
37 https://en.wikipedia.org/wiki/Jimmie_Walker

38 https://en.wikipedia.org/wiki/Bill_Murray
39 https://en.wikipedia.org/wiki/Jeff_Goldblum
40 https://en.wikipedia.org/wiki/Mel_Brooks
41 https://en.wikipedia.org/wiki/Alex_Karras
42 https://en.wikipedia.org/wiki/Ron_Clark_(writer)
43 https://en.wikipedia.org/wiki/Rudy_De_Luca
44 https://en.wikipedia.org/wiki/Barry_Levinson
45 https://en.wikipedia.org/wiki/Marcel_Marceau
46 https://en.wikipedia.org/wiki/Marty_Feldman
47 https://en.wikipedia.org/wiki/Liza_Minnelli
48 https://en.wikipedia.org/wiki/Bernadette_Peters
49 https://en.wikipedia.org/wiki/Sid_Caesar
50 https://en.wikipedia.org/wiki/Carl_Reiner
51 https://en.wikipedia.org/wiki/Richard_Gere
52 https://en.wikipedia.org/wiki/Judith_Rossner
53 https://en.wikipedia.org/wiki/Richard_Brooks
54 https://en.wikipedia.org/wiki/Richard_Kiley
55 https://en.wikipedia.org/wiki/Tuesday_Weld
56 https://en.wikipedia.org/wiki/William_A._Fraker
57 https://en.wikipedia.org/wiki/Richard_Chamberlain
58 https://en.wikipedia.org/wiki/Alexandre_Dumas
59 https://en.wikipedia.org/wiki/Richard_Lester
60 https://en.wikipedia.org/wiki/George_MacDonald_Fraser
61 https://en.wikipedia.org/wiki/Michael_York
62 https://en.wikipedia.org/wiki/Oliver_Reed
63 https://en.wikipedia.org/wiki/Raquel_Welch
64 https://en.wikipedia.org/wiki/Charlie_Sheen
65 https://en.wikipedia.org/wiki/Kiefer_Sutherland
66 https://en.wikipedia.org/wiki/Oliver_Platt
67 https://en.wikipedia.org/wiki/Chris_O%27Donnell
68 https://en.wikipedia.org/wiki/Paul_W._S._Anderson
69 https://en.wikipedia.org/wiki/Luke_Evans
70 https://en.wikipedia.org/wiki/Ray_Stevenson
71 https://en.wikipedia.org/wiki/Milla_Jovovich

VI. Movies I Didn't See...And Glad I Hadn't

The following are John's reviews of movies I don't regret missing and think that John probably wishes he had. Let's dive right in.

Did you know that Brooke Shields[1] began her career as a baby in an Ivory soap ad? (No, she wasn't the Gerber baby as was rumored for years.) She then went on to be a child model until she got a role for a movie at the ripe old age of twelve. The flick created a stir since it was reminiscent of *Lolita*,[2] meaning an adult male was nothing more than a creepy pedophile taking advantage of a child. In this case it was *Pretty Baby* (1978).

Just Another Pretty Face (and Another, and Another)

By John Barbour

Louis is Malle-Functioning

Twelve-year-old Brook Shields has the kind of hauntingly beautiful face that could launch a thousand movies. But a movie, like beauty, must be more than skin deep. Unfortunately, in *Pretty Baby* director Louis Malle[3] seems so fascinated with that face that he lets his camera linger on it endlessly, creating great photographs but a lousy movie. As a matter of fact, he has taken a dynamite premise—that of a 12-year-old virgin who lives in a 1917 New Orleans whorehouse and aspires to follow in her mother's mattresses—and turned it into a film so dull it would bore even Roman Polanski.[4] For all the emotion it elicits we might as well have been watching young Brooke eat a Big Mac.

When Malle isn't photographing Shields' face, he's photographing Keith Carradine[5] photographing her mother's (Susan Sarandon's[6]) breasts—and, as they say, if you've seen two you've seen them all. Carradine plays a photographer who comes to the cathouse to take pictures of hookers and eventually falls in love with and marries Shields. He looks like an emaciated Toulouse-Lautrec[7] with legs, and his character, like all the others in the film, has no more substance or depth than a tripod. Nobody in the movie has any desires, ambitions, fears or interests and, as a result, we have no interest in them. Despite the fact that the brothel is within a month or so of being closed down by the local league of decency, the girls and the madam seem no more put out by this than if somebody had stolen their soap.

I had never seen Frances Faye[8] in a film. Now that I've seen her play the madam, I know why. She labors over her lines like someone in desperate need of an Evelyn Wood speed-reading course, and her delivery is a raspy, monotonous singsong that makes her sound like an understudy to Mae West[9] in *Sextette.*

There is, in fact, only one stunning moment in the movie. The opening scene displays a brief burst of imagination and inventiveness that the rest of the film never recaptures. The camera, naturally, is on Shields' face. She is standing at the foot of the bed watching something that sounds like the mounting moaning and groaning of a woman reaching a painfully ecstatic orgasm. But, as Malle later shows us, what she is watching is her mother giving birth, assisted by a black midwife who is so offhandedly casual that she might as well be pulling another turkey out of the oven.

The problem here is that Malle has paid more attention to the authenticity of the sets and period than he has to probing his people. As a result, some moments that should have had enormous emotional impact have virtually none. One such disturbingly benign scene occurs when the madam and the mother auction off the girl's virginity. By the time this takes place we are so numb and indifferent to Shields that for all we care the women could be auctioning off a piece of furniture.

But when Malle takes close shots of the intense, creased, middle-aged male faces ogling the girl something strange happens. While we feel nothing for the plight of the girl, we are captivated by the blank stares of the bidders and wonder what their lives must have been like—what altered ambitions and ruptured dreams would bring them to be part of this perversity. There is something wrong with a film when the eyes of strangers who appear for an instant spark our imaginations more than all the main characters put together do in two hours.

In spite of its pretty pictures and Brook Shields' pretty face, *Pretty Baby* is pretty awful. There's not enough story to make it a halfway decent film, not enough indecency to make it halfway decent porn.

It's no secret that child actors often grow up to be screwed up adults. Two years after *Pretty Baby*, Shields was in the controversial Calvin Klein jeans commercial where she suggestively posed and says: "Do you know what comes between me and my Calvins? Nothing."

Following that, she made a couple teen movies but then attended Princeton University and got a degree in Romance Languages. She then went back to a successful career in acting and seems to have managed to overcome many of the obstacles that did in many other child actors. I do wonder, though, if being in such a mature-themed movie did something to her overall wellbeing. So I asked John the following question: "Do you have or did you have any thoughts on children playing such roles as Brooke Shields did in *Pretty Baby* and Linda Blair[10] did in *The Exorcist*? Did you think critiquing their performances would be difficult because they were children?"

His reply was short and to the point: "As for kids, some are brilliant performers who often steal a film. Linda Blair in *Exorcist* and Jody Foster[11] in *Alice Doesn't Live Here Anymore,* and especially Natalie Portman[12] in *The Professional.* It could not have been the great gangster film it was without her performance. But no child will ever equal the all-around talent of Shirley Temple[13]!"

I agree about Shirley Temple, although when she became a teenager I felt her ability to capture an audience had been compromised simply because she grew up and was not the precocious, tap-dancing charmer any longer. But here's a good place to share another movie that I purposely missed.

I'd read *The Exorcist* by William Peter Blatty[14] when it came out. I could turn the pages or put the book down if it got too intense or frightening but I knew that going to see the movie would certainly be too disturbing for me. Then *Exorcist II: The Heretic* came out in 1977. Again, I had no interest in creeping myself out. I don't think it creeped John out, but it certainly did disturb him:

Watching Richard Burton,[15] Linda Blair and Louise Fletcher[16] in *Exorcist II: The Heretic* is like a reversal on an old Jackie Mason[17] joke: When Jackie started out in show business, he said he once followed an act that was so bad that during his *own* act they were still booing the other guy. Well, John Boorman's[18] sequel is so bad that just by association it will cause audiences to boo the memory of William Friedkin.[19] There is so much ineptness stuffed into this that it overflows and infects the original.

From the opening credits you get the feeling you are about to watch one of the worst movies ever made. Over a black screen with red credits we hear what is supposed to be spooky chanting: what it sounds like, though, is six rabbis and a cantor with food poisoning at a bar mitzvah. And the storyline is such a hodgepodge that not even the Brushy Mountain bloodhounds who caught James Earl Ray[20] could follow it.

From the scent that I was able to pick up, it seems that Blair is going to a psychiatrist—there's nothing wrong with her, but her mother is afraid one day she may have bad dreams about her childhood possession. Meanwhile, Burton, a priest, is sent from Rome to investigate the death of Father Merrin, who died during the girl's exorcism. As a priest, Burton feels unworthy; as an actor in this, he most certainly is—he is possessed by so much ham he should be exorcised from the Screen Actors Guild by Farmer John. As for Fletcher, as Blair's psychiatrist she should send back her Oscar for *Cuckoo's Nest* with an abject apology.

Anyway, to find out what's in the girl's mind, Burton and Fletcher take turns wiring the girl and themselves to some Rube Goldberg[21] contraption that allows them to see Blair's buried memories. What they see and what we see is that the girl is no longer possessed by the Devil—but by a giant grasshopper. This grasshopper flies to Africa where it joins a bunch of other grasshoppers, and while Max Von Sydow[22] watches, they eat a corn field and a little black boy for dessert. The bug's spirit grows up to become James Earl Jones[23], one of Africa's leading bug specialists and a good witch doctor. After *this*, it gets confusing. The boy eaten in this film is much better off than anyone watching it.

In a desperate attempt to salvage this grasshopper-turkey, Warner Bros. was re-editing the film and tacking on a new ending while the first version was still running in theaters. The only possible way that audiences will sit long enough to see that new ending is if Warner's puts the new ending at the beginning. Before the credits.

Sometimes one scene can be enough to get people talking about a movie, and there's much to be said for word of mouth when it comes to selling tickets. With that in mind, I cannot help but think of *Deliverance* and that one disturbing scene, accompanied by *Dueling Banjos*, a tune that will forever be associated with it. In 1972 when the movie came out, I knew enough that made me steer clear of it. Then, years later, when it aired on TV, I still avoided it. After reading John's review, I don't regret it.

Ronny Cox[24], *Ned Beatty*[25], *Burt Reynolds, Jon Voight*[26]

In case you're not too interested in seeing one of the many films around where a man rapes a woman, or in case you're not too interested in seeing *Portnoy's Complaint* where a man rapes his hand, Warner Bros. offers an alternative in *Deliverance*. Now you can see a man rape a man. This affectionate moment occurs about forty minutes after the credits. I tell you this because in *Deliverance*, this is also where what story there is really begins.

Up until this moment in the film we have journeyed with four relatively uninteresting and characterless men, played some hill people to drive their vehicles back down the mountains, and are on the last canoe ride down a Georgia backcountry river that will soon be part of a lake created by another of man's reservoirs.

Burt Reynolds is the outdoorsy leader. We can tell this because he has lines like "you can't beat the river" and "someday the forest will win," which he delivers as if he really wished he were riding down the rapids on Johnny Carson's couch. We can also tell because he wears a navel-length Harry Belafonte[27] V-neck and carries a bow and arrow, looking like the August centerfold of *Field and Stream*.

When two of Burt's party are taken captive by a pair of sadistic and grubby mountain men and are sexually assaulted and debased, I am sure director John Boorman and author James Dickey[28] meant somehow to show us the Human Condition, to show us something about justice, the law of the jungle, the laws of civilization, and the survival of the fittest. Like many others, though, I've simply become weary of seeing those subjects expressed through lacerated human skin and abused human genitals.

There is no questioning the impact of the rape scene; there is also no questioning of its repulsiveness. The audience is perhaps even glad when Burt saves his friends from further degradation by putting an arrow through the back of one of the assailants. However, when he talks about dismembering and hiding the various parts of the corpse, even though it is obviously justifiable homicide, he becomes not much different from his victim. One brutalizing the living; the other brutalizing the dead. And whatever empathy we might have felt for the other three is lost when, along with the discourse on how to dispose of the body, they indulge in a forced, high school debate on democracy and society. Even the cadaver was overacting, leaning bug-eyed against a tree, as though he couldn't believe what he was hearing.

Following this moment there is a certain amount of tension, wondering if the mountain man who escaped will reappear. But like politics, it becomes a question of pulling for the lesser of two evils.

I have to admit, as disturbing as this movie is, John's comment about Burt riding the rapids on Johnny Carson's couch made me laugh out loud. He (John) certainly knew how to jibe Burt.

Growing up, I recall watching Bob Hope specials while not recalling finding him particularly funny. But because programming was limited where I was raised, it was mild entertainment that went along with my bowl of popcorn on a weeknight when there was not much else to do. And as for Hope's "Road" movies, I only saw parts of them when they aired on television and wasn't pulled in enough to keep watching. In 1972, Bob Hope made the last of his movies, some fifty in all, as a leading man. John reviewed it.

Why Bob Hope Isn't Funny Anymore

By John Barbour

It's hard to make people laugh when you've become a $500 million corporation—and an institution

For Bob Hope, a very unfunny thing happened on the way to the peace table. It's called *Cancel My Reservation.*

Bob Hope plays Bob Hope playing Dan Bartlett, the host of a successful TV talk show. After an argument with his wife, Eva Marie Saint[29], over her getting more public recognition since joining him on the show, *Hope goes West*; there he accidentally gets involved in some murders.

In order to make himself look young in this thing, Hope seems to have cast most of the parts from the waiting list for Forest Lawn. And in order to show how spry he still is, he stuck Ralph Bellamy[30] in a wheel chair. Bing Crosby[31] was even revived long enough to do his usual one line cameo: for a moment we thought we were watching *The Road to Leisure World.* There were more lines on the faces than there were in the script. It was all so phony it had me questioning the honesty of anything in the film; I found myself looking at Anne Archer[32], a pretty young actress with a fantastic chest, and wondering whether or not her nose was real.

After watching *Cancel my Reservation*, I am forced to admit to myself that there is no such thing as a new Bob Hope movie; only new titles, and perhaps the real title of this should be: *Everything You Always Knew Was Wrong With Bob Hope, But Were Afraid to Say*. Until now.

I'm like most people of my generation: When I was a youngster, one of my heroes was Bob Hope. The Second World War was on, and I couldn't wait for that night once a week when I'd sit in front of the radio with the faded orange and yellow dial, listen to the orchestra play "Thanks for the Memory," and crack up at the sound of Hope saying, "Hi, this is Bob Broadcasting from Camp Pendleton Hope." Through two wars, Korea (which the government referred to as a Police Action) and Vietnam (which the government refers to as little as possible). Bob Hope became an institution. He was the funny Voice of America.

In a day and age, though, when we are being forced to question our political and social institutions, maybe we should also be questioning some of our outdated entertainment institutions; for me, for the past few years, it has been easier to question our government than it has been to question Bob Hope. We have, for the most part, been involved with the government only with our wallets, but in growing up with Hope, we became involved with our hearts. Out of old loyalties and happy boyhood recollections, I still found myself wanting to go to Bob Hope movies, and staying home to watch his TV specials.

The more I see him now, though, in films and on TV, the more I realize with Hope it is truly Thanks For the Memory, because sad to say, in this tired movie and his terrible TV shows, there is nothing presently to be thankful for. One of Hope's strong points in the past was his material. In *Cancel My Reservation* that's where a lot of it came from... the past. He even did voice-over narration and gags...perhaps because he thought he was doing radio again. He now sounds like a gentile

Henny Youngman[33], and delivers his material with all the verve of Eric Sevareid.[34] He's become, regrettably, the J. Edgar Hoover[35] of humor.

Even though I still want to listen to him, I find he doesn't communicate. And maybe he doesn't communicate because he has nothing to say. He is a one-line joke man. That is the depth of his conviction; and after all these years it seems also to be the depth of his personality. As a topical gag-teller, he'll hang jokes on headlines, but you never get the feeling he has read or even understood the story inside. A real humorist has. And a humorist has a point of view about that story as a human being. Hope has the point of view of a Corporation.

Hope deserves respect for the length of time he has managed to survive and remain a force in this soul-destroying business; he deserves honor for the amount of known and unknown charitable work he has done, but in a world that desperately needs some real humor, he is no longer funny. Emotional and financial and intellectual hunger are the bastard parents of a comedian, and maybe it is difficult to strive to make people honestly laugh when you've become beloved by millions, and are a $500 million corporation—and an Institution.

Bob Hope would do himself well, and his audience well, if he would retire as Chairman of the Board…before the existing realities of his present work begins outweighing some of those still pleasant memories.

This was stunning for me to read and I imagine it offended a lot of people, because as John states, Bob Hope was an institution. As I copied John's review of *Cancel My Reservation* for this book, which was more a review of the comedian than the movie, I spotted the following on the bottom of the *LA Magazine* page:

John Barbour appears as KTTV's humorous critic-at-large Monday, Wednesday and Friday evenings on the 10 p.m. MetroNews.

Had I had access to that, I would have made it my business to watch religiously. The very idea that he could review movies with such wit and humor would have been as entertaining as the movie itself—at least for me.

Notes

1 https://en.wikipedia.org/wiki/Brooke_Shields
2 https://en.wikipedia.org/wiki/Lolita
3 https://en.wikipedia.org/wiki/Louis_Malle
4 https://en.wikipedia.org/wiki/Roman_Polanski
5 https://en.wikipedia.org/wiki/Keith_Carradine
6 https://en.wikipedia.org/wiki/Susan_Sarandon
7 https://en.wikipedia.org/wiki/Henri_de_Toulouse-Lautrec
8 https://en.wikipedia.org/wiki/Frances_Faye
9 https://en.wikipedia.org/wiki/Mae_West
10 https://en.wikipedia.org/wiki/Linda_Blair
11 https://en.wikipedia.org/wiki/Jodie_Foster
12 https://en.wikipedia.org/wiki/Natalie_Portman
13 https://en.wikipedia.org/wiki/Shirley_Temple
14 https://en.wikipedia.org/wiki/William_Peter_Blatty
15 https://en.wikipedia.org/wiki/Richard_Burton
16 https://en.wikipedia.org/wiki/Louise_Fletcher
17 https://en.wikipedia.org/wiki/Jackie_Mason
18 https://en.wikipedia.org/wiki/John_Boorman
19 https://en.wikipedia.org/wiki/William_Friedkin
20 https://en.wikipedia.org/wiki/James_Earl_Ray
21 https://en.wikipedia.org/wiki/Rube_Goldberg_machine
22 https://en.wikipedia.org/wiki/Max_von_Sydow
23 https://en.wikipedia.org/wiki/James_Earl_Jones
24 https://en.wikipedia.org/wiki/Ronny_Cox
25 https://en.wikipedia.org/wiki/Ned_Beatty
26 https://en.wikipedia.org/wiki/Jon_Voight
27 https://en.wikipedia.org/wiki/Harry_Belafonte
28 https://en.wikipedia.org/wiki/James_Dickey
29 https://en.wikipedia.org/wiki/Eva_Marie_Saint
30 https://en.wikipedia.org/wiki/Ralph_Bellamy
31 https://en.wikipedia.org/wiki/Bing_Crosby
32 https://en.wikipedia.org/wiki/Anne_Archer
33 https://en.wikipedia.org/wiki/Henny_Youngman
34 https://en.wikipedia.org/wiki/Eric_Sevareid
35 https://en.wikipedia.org/wiki/J._Edgar_Hoover

VII. John Reviews Other Reviewers' Reviews

It takes a certain kind of hubris to actually critique other reviewers' reviews. When I was in the middle of writing this book, I received the following email from John:

Carol: good morning. Just a thought and memory for you, but maybe not for your book. During the 70's when my son was a 3-to-9 year-old golf prodigy, I took him daily to the Studio City driving range to hit balls. You'd be astounded at how many actors and writers, known and unknown, thanked me for my reviews. They said they wished that they could say the things I said about films and the business, and always ended asking how on earth I kept my job. In looking at all the stuff I sent you, one of the pieces I enjoyed reading the most, but not remembering writing it was my critique of other critics. I was stunned I was that ballsy and independent! (A loner since birth, I guess.) Also, there was an LA association of critics that I declined to join in order to maintain my independence. Hugs. John.

Well, I have to say that John's article titled *The 10 Worst Film Reviews of the Year* had to have raised those hackles but after reading it, it is just too entertaining not to include in this book. Enjoy.

Gobble your popcorn through this one, Rex Reed[1].

Being a film critic is a bastard art in that you can't always talk about someone else's art or lack of it without occasionally feeling like a bastard. But that doesn't stop me. It also doesn't stop me from knocking other critics from time to time, and my editors always worry that some people might consider that unethical or, at the least, in bad taste.

As a result, I've decided to kick this column off by knocking my employers too in order to demonstrate my sense of fair play. Now, our esteemed editor, Geoff Miller, might think it a little tacky of me to bite the hand that feeds me, but what he feeds me doesn't have to be held in his hand. A finger would suffice. As a result of its being too small to sink my teeth into, and because I have a slight overbite anyway, when he holds it out every month for me to nibble on, my teeth have nowhere else to go. You can always tell when it's the day after Geoff has paid his writers: His fist is covered with Band-Aids.

Now that I've shown that I'm not above poking a little honest fun at my own boss, that cheap bastard, I'd like to talk about a couple of fellow critics' reviews that also cost me—and I'm sure, a lot of other people—some money.

The public reads and listens to critics for two reasons: for entertainment and for information. There are only a handful of critics in this country whose judgments and values I respect, and fewer still whose wit and intelligence I admire. I'd rather read a differing view of a film by a bright critic whose style is superior than one by a bore whose opinions I agree with. To those of an opposite political persuasion, the ideas of William Buckley[2] and Gore Vidal[3] are saved from the philosophical dung heap by a cutting, elegant wit that transforms those thoughts, even in the view of their detractors, into funny mental fertilizer. Unfortunately, in many major newspapers—and especially in TV—there are too many critics who are listened to not because they know how to write or how to be honest, but simply because they are there. These are the soulless, humorless ones who are called *critic* only by their employers.

The one exception in television, now that I have removed myself from channel 4 because the folks there, too, were cheap bastards, is Gene Shalit, who continually demonstrates a flair for the language and an affection for films. However, for the public, the bottom line is that a critic be a reliable, articulate tour guide to places where the reader or listener should spend his or her entertainment dollar. Often this past year I went to movies that fellow critics claimed would be the most magical cinematic trip since Dorothy skipped into Emerald City, only to wind up feeling as if I were trapped in Uganda. So instead of compiling a 10-worst-films list for 1978, I have compiled a list of the 10 worst, most misleading reviews of 1978. They are:

(1) Pauline Kael's review of *Invasion of the Body Snatchers* in the *New Yorker.* In describing this film as "the best movie of its kind ever made… an American classic," Kael indicates that in a book she wrote a number of years ago called *I lost It at the Movies* she must have been referring to her taste.

(2) Rex Reed's review of *Superman* in the New York *Daily News*. Rex's first acting role was as Myron in the excessive *Myra Breckenridge*. Following a comeback cameo appearance playing himself in *Superman*—and in keeping with the no-conflict-of-interest class he displayed in doing a commercial for a TV manufacturer—he stated objectively that *Superman* was a "marvel of stupendous filmmaking," proving that as a reviewer he is even less believable than as an actor.

(3) Andrew Sarris'[4] review of *Magic* in the *Village Voice*. Anyone who says that "*Magic* is the most intelligent kind of filmmaking this side of inspiration" shouldn't be writing for the *Village Voice* but for the *Village Idiot*.

(4) Gene Shalit's review of *Movie Movie* on NBC. Shalit called *Movie Movie* one of the funniest films he'd seen in a long time; sitting next to Tom Brokaw two hours a day, anything must seem hilarious.

(5) Charles Champlin's review of *Days of Heaven* in the *L.A. Times*. In placing *Days of Heaven* near the top of his 10-best list, Champlin declared that "the purity of the film more than made up for a certain coolness and an occasional confusion." When it comes to writing about

films, Champlin's confusion is not occasional. It is chronic.

(6) Jack Kroll's[5] review of *Comes a Horseman* in *Newsweek*. Kroll wrote, "It's good to see so much sensitivity amidst the sagebrush…finding truth in light!" He should quit being influenced by Charles Champlin; all anybody else saw in the film was the sagebrush and the darkness.

(7) Richard Schickel's[6] review of *Hooper* in *Time*. Schickel called *Hooper* a really good movie in which "Robert Klein (with) his round face and soft body gives a fine-tuned comic performance of a man-boy." Schickel should quit being influenced by Kevin Thomas; nobody else is.

(8) Rex Reed's review of *The Wiz*. (Yes, Reed again.) Not only did he describe it as "colossal entertainment," but in reviewing the cast he wrote, "Everybody is just plain perfect." With writing ability and taste like that, Hollywood could make Reed its ambassador to Billy Carter.[7]

(9) Stephen Farber's[8] review of *The Deer Hunter* in *New West*. Farber said this film, "which has affected me more profoundly than any,...will last." It *does* last—over three hours. But then Farber goes on to say, "We're involved and sympathetic, but keep our distance," you don't know whether he's talking about a movie or a new disco step.

(10) Rex Reed's review of *Moment by Moment*. That does it. All but Reed and Kevin Thomas[9] found this dreadful film to be to entertainment what Preparation H is to advanced medicine. Saying it is "a funny, warm and wonderfully romantic film" is Reed's third strike, after at least 14 foul balls. If the New York *Daily News* and the motion-picture industry don't gong him, they should take up a collection and send him and David Sheehan[10] to Sweden, where they could be operated on and turned into credible critics.

After putting these critiques on the page, I sent the following email to John:

Oh my, I am still laughing after copying the list into the book! But I have to ask, did any of those reviewers respond to your critiques of them, especially Rex Reed? Too funny!

John replied, "*None ever contacted me. But I may have mentioned the wife of the LA Times critic called screaming obscenities at my after I said he never met a starlet he did not like.*"

Notes

1 https://en.wikipedia.org/wiki/Rex_Reed
2 https://en.wikipedia.org/wiki/William_F._Buckley_Jr.
3 https://en.wikipedia.org/wiki/Gore_Vidal
4 https://en.wikipedia.org/wiki/Andrew_Sarris
5 https://en.wikipedia.org/wiki/Jack_Kroll
6 https://en.wikipedia.org/wiki/Richard_Schickel
7 https://en.wikipedia.org/wiki/Billy_Carter
8 https://www.rottentomatoes.com/critic/stephen-farber/movies
9 https://en.wikipedia.org/wiki/Kevin_Thomas_(film_critic)
10 https://en.wikipedia.org/wiki/David_Sheehan

VIII. Currently Showing

In the stacks of reviews that John sent, there was also a sidebar with brief reviews of movies that were, well, currently showing. Even though his comments were only a couple of sentences, they were still as witty as the longer reviews. And, I have to say, I am not familiar with a large number of these movie titles, but you might be surprised like I was, by how many of these John enjoyed, which makes me want to watch out for them when they will possibly air on Turner Classics or PBS. I'm not listing these by the year they came out, but alphabetically.

Avanti—Jack Lemmon and a calorie counting Juliette Mills[1] are perfect in this very enjoyable film about an American husband and an English boutique owner who journey to Italy to retrieve the bodies of his father and her mother. It has all the right and light Billy Wilder[2] touches.

Bluebeard should have its rating changed from "R" to "PG" for Piece of Garbage. If Richard Burton turns up in one more abomination like this, he won't even be able to buy Liz zircons. He is now to the point where he deserves a leading lady such as he has in Bluebeard: Joey Heatherton.[3]

Cabaret—Liza Minnelli is a marvelously musical Sally Bowles and Joel Grey[4] repeats his superb Broadway role as the M.C. to make this a dazzling adaptation of the Isherwood[5] stories of pre-war Berlin.

The Candidate—An extraordinary film by any standards. Director Michael Ritchie[6] achieves an uncanny verisimilitude as his handheld cameras hound first-time senatorial candidate Robert Redford through his grueling, uphill campaign in California. Redford is so good you may be tempted to write him in, come November.

Child's Play—An unbelievable and tedious religious allegory in which the audience dies for David Merrick's[7] sins. James Mason's brilliant performance as the Latin teacher who cannot cope with what is supposed to be a growing terror and evil amongst some of the students in a Catholic boarding school is wasted. So is your time. Robert Preston[8] as his conniving nemesis looks like he's glad he can still get a job singing and dancing.

A Clockwork Orange—Writer-producer-director Stanley Kubrick's mastery of his art is displayed in bravura style in his multi-level adaptation of Anthony Burgess's's[9] futuristic novel. It is a harrowing vision of tomorrow, a deeply engrossingly and vastly entertaining work. For once, the sex and violence have validity.

Coonskin—Ralph Bakshi's[10] Br'er Rabbit fable—in which the residents of Harlem rip one another off—pounds the audience over the head with the obvious. Instead of touching the soul, the shallow characters just get under your skin.

Cries and Whispers—Superior performances and photography don't exactly help lighten the mood of this Ingmar Bergman[11] downer about a couple of sisters and a housekeeper hanging around the house waiting for another sister to die. In an early scene, one of the sisters doesn't want to have sex with her husband so she takes a broken wine glass and mutilates herself, then smears the blood on her face. Wouldn't a simple "no" have been just as effective?

The Culpepper Cattle Co.—A teenaged, would-be cowboy's coming of age during a cattle drive with the grungiest bunch of sidewinders that ever stove a dung-encrusted boot into a longhorn's hind end. Cast and settings look as authentic as a Remington[12] painting.

Day of the Jackal—The Violence is handled brilliantly in this crisp, engrossing Fred Zinnemann[13] film about a plot to assassinate DeGaulle.[14] Most of it is anticipated or implied, making it all the more terrifying. Edward Fox[15] as the Jackal and Michel Lonsdale[16] as the frumpy French detective tracking him are perfect.

Duck, You Sucker—With a title like that, this would figure to be a slapstick comedy about the movie business, but as we've long since learned, Sergio Leone[17] gets his chuckles from carnage. This time it's an endless, if spotty, history of the Mexican Revolution, with oppressive emoting by Rod Steiger[18] as a dusty bandito and a lot of fang-baring by James Coburn[19] as an exiled IRA bomber.

The Garden of the Finzi-Continis—Vittorio de Sica's[20] finest film in years is a beautiful and heart-rending examination of people unsuspectingly on the brink of annihilation, in this instance an aristocratic family of Jews in the Italy of the late '30s.

Hard Times—Like an old-time Western hero, Charles Bronson plays a Depression street fighter who drift into town on a boxcar with $6 and a face that looks like boxcars have been riding on it. He teams up with a misfit promoter, James Coburn, and the result is a simple, yet effective film with Bronson at his best as an actor—because he isn't given much to say.

Hitler: The Last Ten Days—A disturbingly shallow film in which the barbarism of the Second World War and the man who precipitated it are inadvertently made to appear somehow less repugnant.

Junior Bonner—Sam Peckinpah's predictably callous brawler about the rodeo, with Steve McQueen as the two-fisted Junior, a champeen[21] bronc-buster who goes back home to visit his folks and finds out they've gotten to be a pretty sorry pair by this time.

Kansas City Bomber—The best thing in this film is Raquel Welch roller skating, which she does about as gracefully as Ironsides.[22] As an actress Raquel has yet to get the part that could best showcase what she has to offer. When that picture comes along, she will be eaten by a giant squid within the first ten seconds before she opens her mouth.

Last of the Red-Hot Lovers—Barney Cashman (Alan Arkin[23]) is a rank amateur when it comes to adultery and, depending on which of three neurotic ladies he is trying to seduce, this Neil Simon comedy is at times very funny indeed. Sally Kellerman[24] and Paula Prentiss[25] make the most of their roles in unconsummated affairs #1 and #2, but Renee Taylor[26] is so strident and disagreeable as #3, we find ourselves hoping Arkin will either mend his ways or take up tie-murdering.

Let's Do It Again—Even though this plot about a couple of guys (Bill Cosby[27] and Sidney Poitier) hypnotizing a puny fighter to the point where he thinks he's the Gorilla from Manila[28]—all for a good cause—is as old as Joe E. Brown[29] and Abbott and Costello[30], it is paced and performed with a zest that seems both fresh and refreshing. And as the puny fighter, J.J. Walker is as funny as he is ugly.

The Master Gunfighter—Tom Laughlin[31] has made a pseudo-sociological western which he calls half fiction and half fact but which is really half assed. With all the bad guys carrying samurai swords that Laughlin takes on, it would be laughable if it weren't so insulting: the Indians he's trying to help are made to look like a bunch of passive Uncle Tom-Toms just sitting around waiting for this superior white man to save them.

Money, Money, Money—Claude Lelouch has made one of the funniest films you'll see in years. Five middle-aged, bright-but-bumbling thieves give up robbing banks to learn about politics so they can *really* steal, and after a series of ingenious comic kidnappings and hijackings become Revolutionary heroes.

Money Talks—Allen Funt[32] is to films what Tiny Tim[33] is to music. He had a great gimmick that he should have given up on when *Candid Camera* went into its fifth rerun. The premise of *Money Talks* is that people will do dumb things when it comes to money; and Allen Funt proves it with this dumb picture.

Murmur of the Heart—A French film that deals with incest, in this instance of the Oedipal persuasion. It's all perfectly OK, though, because the son is bedded down with this heart murmur and Mom really loves the kid. You have to be awfully sophisticated to really appreciate, or ignore, this logic, however. Degenerates, incidentally, will be sadly disappointed.

The Neptune Factor—An unbelievably amateurish movie about two unbelievable aquanauts, Ernie Borgnine[34] and Ben Gazzara[35], who search the ocean floor for a lost sea lab—not to mention the script. It should be retitled *Journey to the Bottom of the Barrel.* If Ernie is in physical shape to be an aquanaut, Mama Cass[36] is a toe-dancer.

The New Centurions—When George C. Scott[37] wasn't showing up to accept his awards, he certainly couldn't have been home reading this script. To get an idea of what you'll see, put a Belle Barth[38] or Moms Mabley[39] L.P. on your turntable[40], then turn into reruns of *Adam 12.* The cardboard characters in the film should be taken down to the Police Academy and used for target practice.

The Other—Almost unbearably true to Thomas Tryon's[41] best-selling tale of two spooky ten-year-old twin boys who have a way of getting into spine-tingling trouble, including a series of ghastly fatalities. Director Robert Mulligan, just the man for the job, recalls much of his *Mockingbird* mood and handles a heavy tapestry of small-town characters, brooding symbols, Depression-era paraphernalia and sheer gothic horror with a grace and facility that is itself pretty frightening.

Paper Moon—A charming, black-and-white film by Peter Bogdanovich[42] set in the thirties. While conman and Bible salesman Moses Pray (Ryan O'Neal) is stealing money from all the widows in Kansas and Missouri, Addie (Tatum O'Neal[43]), his nine-year old orphaned accomplice is hustling the hearts of the audience.

Pat Garrett and Billy the Kid—Sam Peckinpah's talents have gone to the Straw Dogs. The best thing about this tedious film, in which the script is as meaningless as the slaughter, is Bob Dylan's[44] music; and that's awful. Both are about as western as velvet Levis and Dylan sings and acts as though he had a mouthful of saddle.

Pete 'n' Tillie—The first half of this comedy-drama about courtship and marriage works better that the second half. Perhaps that's because everybody knows what seduction is about, but few can figure out what marriage is about. Walter Matthau and Carol Burnett[45] are very good, and Geraldine Page[46] handles a scene in which she cannot reveal her age brilliantly. But if anything holds this film together, it is some of the eminently quotable lines, funny and thoughtful, that Julius Epstein[47] has put into the characters' mouths.

Play It As It Lays—If you must go to see this depressing film, take a friend: Librium. Were Oscar Levant[48] still alive he might have enjoyed Tuesday Weld's character, finding solace in watching the suffering of someone worse off than he ever was.

Portnoy's Complaint—Writer-director Ernest Lehman[49] gives us the impression that the way to a man's heart is through his groin. He leaves Portnoy lingering there because there is no heart in this film to go to. It was left in Philip Roth's[50] novel…along with the funnybone.

The Possession of Joel Delaney—Shirley MacLaine's[51] kid brother starts babbling like the devil in Spanish and it turns out he's possessed by the spirit of a teenaged Puerto Rican murderer. What the audience doesn't realize is that director Waris Hussein[52] is possessed by the spirit of a senile, semi-retired Polish hog butcher.

Prime Cut—Lee Marvin[53], a mob enforcer, goes to Kansas to shoot some sense into Gene Hackman's[54] boys who have been acting up lately. Most of the bloodshed takes place under surrealistic circumstances amid the sunflowers and the wheat fields. The plot has all the probability (and substance) of a comic book.

The Public Eye—For some reason there is a preoccupation here with food and eating; probably because they had to put something in the actors' mouths to take away the bland taste of the dialogue. Hal Wallis[55] is the cook, Carol Reed[56] is the caterer, Mia Farrow is the waitress, and what they serve is goulash.

Roma—Federico Fellini[57] has put together a self-indulgent, pointless travelogue about the Eternal City which proves that even gifted artists shouldn't play with themselves in public. Not only is the Fellini touch missing, it doesn't have the Fitzpatrick touch.

Rooster Cogburn—John Wayne as the hard-drinking, two-fisted, one-eyed renegade lawman looks like he tried to act for the first time in films and ends up sounding like Wallace Beery.[58] When he is on the screen with Kate Hepburn, the film glows; however, when they're not together, they and the audience could watch the rest of this empty movie with patches over *both* eyes.

Scarecrow—Two fine performances by Al Pacino and Gene Hackman can't salvage this depressing tedious film about two bums whose big ambition in life is to get to Pittsburgh.

A Separate Peace—The only thing worse than a lead character who does nothing (e.g. Tuesday Weld in *Play it…*) is one who spends all his time thinking about something he shouldn't have done. For a man to build a lifetime around the memory of pushing his school chum out of a tree is bad living. The film that Larry Peerce[59] built around it is bad art. The teenaged characters who people it should all have been pushed out of a tree.

Skyjacked—Lord knows MGM can use the money, but unless you're feeling charitable or you happen to have liked *Airport*, your best bet is to stay off this flight.

Slaughterhouse Five—Under George Roy Hill's direction, the Kurt Vonnegut[60] novel becomes a collage of anarchic relationships between time and space. At the same time it is an immensely humane film, with a loving, sympathetic view towards generations, losers and lost ideals.

Sounder—A warm and gentle film about a Southern sharecropper's family and their dog. Some excellent performances and nice subtle touches by director Martin Ritt[61], but *Sounder* doesn't seem to warrant quite the acclaim it is getting; it's not much more than Lassie[62] in blackface.

State of Siege—In this heavy-handed examination of American police involvement in assassinating and torturing Latin American activists, Costa-Gavras[63] overlooks the lessons he should have learned from *The Battle of Algiers*—probably the best movie with a political theme ever made. This time, he puts politics before people, and the audience to sleep.

Ten from Your Show of Shows—We now have to pay to see in a theatre what we used to see for nothing on TV. But consider the admission price a small residual payment to Sid Caesar *et al* for those years of free pleasure when his must-see *Show of Shows* brought even honeymoons to a standstill.

Three Days of the Condor—When Robert Redford, a CIA reader, discovers there's a CIA within the CIA that the CIA doesn't know about, one of these CIAs guns down his coworkers; and, even though he's next, Redford *still* takes time out in this cluttered, confusing film to make love to Faye Dunaway. She's good, but nobody's *that* good—and neither is this film.

The War Between Men and Women—A non-leering adult comedy inspired by James Thurber's[64] words and pictures. Jack Lemmon, Barbara Harris[65] and Jason Robards wage the battle, along with some animated versions of Thurberesque adversaries. Those who fondly remember TV's short-lived *My World and Welcome To It* will recognize the same touch, applied deftly by the same creators.

A Warm December—Sidney Poitier has made a luke-warm film about an American superdoctor who meets an African superchick who was beauty, brains, money, and a fatal illness. These are all perfect ingredients for an artificially sweetened *Guess Who's Coming to Love Story*?

What's Up, Doc?—Light and foolish fun that frequently attains high hilarity of the sort that went out of style for about 30 years ago, along with the irrelevance. Barbra Streisand and Ryan O'Neal are an improbably match, but they cavort divertingly around San Francisco under the versatile direction of Peter Bogdanovich.

The Valachi Papers—Unlike the Pentagon Papers, these should have been kept secret and Dino Di Laurentis[66] should be brought to trial for making them public. Charles Bronson is okay as Charles Bronson, but the Screen Actors Guild should put out a contract on Joseph Wiseman[67], who portrays a Cosa Nostra leader as though he were auditioning for *Life with Luigi*.

Young Winston—Although we all know what happened to Winston Churchill[68] the politician, a really good film about him as a young man should contain some insight and unpredictability. Unfortunately, this effort by a usually very competent Carl Foreman[69] has little of the former and none of the latter. Even the excellent performances by the three principals fail to make it much more interesting than watching the Changing of the Guard: you're more interested in the uniforms than in the people wearing them.

Notes

1 https://en.wikipedia.org/wiki/Juliet_Mills
2 https://en.wikipedia.org/wiki/Billy_Wilder
3 https://en.wikipedia.org/wiki/Joey_Heatherton
4 https://en.wikipedia.org/wiki/Joel_Grey
5 https://en.wikipedia.org/wiki/Christopher_Isherwood
6 https://en.wikipedia.org/wiki/Michael_Ritchie_(film_director)
7 https://en.wikipedia.org/wiki/David_Merrick
8 https://en.wikipedia.org/wiki/Robert_Preston_(actor)
9 https://en.wikipedia.org/wiki/Anthony_Burgess
10 https://en.wikipedia.org/wiki/Ralph_Bakshi
11 https://en.wikipedia.org/wiki/Ingmar_Bergman
12 https://en.wikipedia.org/wiki/Frederic_Remington
13 https://en.wikipedia.org/wiki/Fred_Zinnemann
14 https://en.wikipedia.org/wiki/Charles_de_Gaulle
15 https://en.wikipedia.org/wiki/Edward_Fox_(actor)
16 https://en.wikipedia.org/wiki/Michael_Lonsdale
17 https://en.wikipedia.org/wiki/Sergio_Leone
18 https://en.wikipedia.org/wiki/Rod_Steiger
19 https://en.wikipedia.org/wiki/James_Coburn
20 https://en.wikipedia.org/wiki/Vittorio_De_Sica
21 John spelled champion this way for his review, so I kept it.
22 https://en.wikipedia.org/wiki/Ironside_(1967_TV_series)
23 https://en.wikipedia.org/wiki/Alan_Arkin
24 https://en.wikipedia.org/wiki/Sally_Kellerman
25 https://en.wikipedia.org/wiki/Paula_Prentiss
26 https://en.wikipedia.org/wiki/Ren%C3%A9e_Taylor
27 https://en.wikipedia.org/wiki/Bill_Cosby
28 Muhammad Ali verbally abused Joe Frazier. Ali nicknamed Frazier "The Gorilla", and used this as the basis for the rhyme, "It will be a killa and a thrilla and a chilla when I get the Gorilla in Manila," which he chanted while punching an action-figure-sized gorilla doll.
29 https://en.wikipedia.org/wiki/Joe_E._Brown
30 https://en.wikipedia.org/wiki/Abbott_and_Costello
31 https://en.wikipedia.org/wiki/Tom_Laughlin
32 https://en.wikipedia.org/wiki/Allen_Funt
33 https://en.wikipedia.org/wiki/Tiny_Tim_(musician)
34 https://en.wikipedia.org/wiki/Ernest_Borgnine

35 https://en.wikipedia.org/wiki/Ben_Gazzara
36 https://en.wikipedia.org/wiki/Cass_Elliot
37 https://en.wikipedia.org/wiki/George_C._Scott
38 https://en.wikipedia.org/wiki/Belle_Barth
39 https://en.wikipedia.org/wiki/Moms_Mabley
40 LP (record) Turntable (record player)
41 https://en.wikipedia.org/wiki/Tom_Tryon
42 https://en.wikipedia.org/wiki/Peter_Bogdanovich
43 https://en.wikipedia.org/wiki/Tatum_O%27Neal
44 https://en.wikipedia.org/wiki/Bob_Dylan
45 https://en.wikipedia.org/wiki/Carol_Burnett
46 https://en.wikipedia.org/wiki/Geraldine_Page
47 https://en.wikipedia.org/wiki/Julius_J._Epstein
48 https://en.wikipedia.org/wiki/Oscar_Levant
49 https://en.wikipedia.org/wiki/Ernest_Lehman
50 https://en.wikipedia.org/wiki/Philip_Roth
51 https://en.wikipedia.org/wiki/Shirley_MacLaine
52 https://en.wikipedia.org/wiki/Waris_Hussein
53 https://en.wikipedia.org/wiki/Lee_Marvin
54 https://en.wikipedia.org/wiki/Gene_Hackman
55 https://en.wikipedia.org/wiki/Hal_B._Wallis
56 https://en.wikipedia.org/wiki/Carol_Reed
57 https://en.wikipedia.org/wiki/Federico_Fellini
58 https://en.wikipedia.org/wiki/Wallace_Beery
59 https://www.rottentomatoes.com/celebrity/larry_peerce
60 https://en.wikipedia.org/wiki/Kurt_Vonnegut
61 https://en.wikipedia.org/wiki/Martin_Ritt
62 https://en.wikipedia.org/wiki/Lassie
63 https://en.wikipedia.org/wiki/Costa-Gavras
64 https://en.wikipedia.org/wiki/James_Thurber
65 https://en.wikipedia.org/wiki/Barbara_Harris_(actress)
66 https://en.wikipedia.org/wiki/Dino_De_Laurentiis
67 https://en.wikipedia.org/wiki/Joseph_Wiseman
68 https://en.wikipedia.org/wiki/Winston_Churchill
69 https://en.wikipedia.org/wiki/Carl_Foreman

IX. Reviewing the Academy Awards

In my notes, I wrote myself a reminder to ask John how he felt about the Academy Awards. I was curious if he felt watching them was enjoyable or did he find himself shouting at the television. When I did ask, he wrote back, *I said often…from the Tonys to the Oscars, the entertainment industry has not yet learned how to put on an entertaining, interesting awards show. The only effective Oscar shows was when Bob Hope hosted them. The very best shows were put on by the private Writers Guild Shows.*

But then while going through the stacks of reviews John had sent me, there was a notation he'd written: "John imagines people reviewing the Academy Awards," and in the May 1978 issue, sure enough, readers were given an idea what John thought of that one night a year that seems to stretch out into days. So here it is:

Every year at the Academy Awards members of the industry honor what they feel is Hollywood's best in a TV show that is always the worst. Reviewing this event is about as useless as opening a Schick Center[1] next to Liggett and Myers[2], so I gave it up about two years ago while still at KNBC. Next year I hope to give up watching it. I mean, if Woody Allen, Jason Robards and the others won't even bother to go, why should I bother to look?

When I was at KNBC, one of the few pleasures I had—other than trying to figure out if Bob Abernethy[3] had a different colored gray suit—was hanging around in the film-editing room during the newscast. It was here I realized that America is a nation of great closet critics. It was here I also realized why they call this area the cutting room. When there was no one of authority around, our two-hour newscast would come on and turn this generally quiet group of skilled and semiskilled editors and assistants into a band of howling, outraged Howard Beales.[4] No sooner would Kelly Lange's[5], Paul Moyer's[6], David Horowitz's[7] or Tritia Toyota's[8] face (or, presumably my own) pop up on the screen than they would cut them down with a series of brilliant, caustic one-line critiques that made John Simon[9] sound duller than Jim Brown[10]. I often thought it would make a fabulous two-hour film to silent-tape the newscast and run it in sync with the cutting-room commentary. It was for having thoughts like that that I'm no longer there.

Knowing that Americans possess a genius for speaking their minds when they think nobody is listening—and having made up my mind never to review the Academy Awards again—I decided that instead of writing a review, I would record one. So I went to a bar and listened to the people listening to the show. Here is a partial transcription of what was said by a dozen or so more people who show they are eminently qualified to come out of the closet—either as critics or news-film editors:

"Geez, there's Bob Hope again. He looks good for his age. How old is he?"

"I dunno. I think about eight wars."

"How'd you like to be directing this thing? The poor guy's gotta find shots of people in the audience laughing."

"Why is John Travolta wearing a scarf?"

"It's the first time he's worn a tuxedo. Maybe he thinks it's a tie."

"What the hell is Vanessa Redgrave[11] saying?"

"She's selling Israeli War Bonds."

"That's all we need—an English Sacheen Littlefeather."

"There's Mickey Mouse."

"The whole show is Mickey Mouse."

"Who is that girl with Paul Williams[12]?"

"Jodie Foster."

"Who is she?"

"She was the girl in *Paper Moon*, wasn't she?"

"No, that was Ryan O'Neal's daughter."

"Why didn't Paul Williams introduce her?"

"Maybe because the mouse and the kid are bigger than he is."

"Christ, if I hear Debby Boone[13] sing 'You Light up My Life' one more time, I'm gonna puke."

"I heard she learns one song for every one of her fathers; and she's only got one father."

"That's kind of a nice touch, though. Those kids accompanying her in sign language."

"They're called the Mormon Tabernacle Fingers."

"Are they really deaf?"

"They must be to keep a straight face."

"How old is Barbara Stanwyck[14]?"

"How old is Bill Holden[15]?"

"What was that terrific war movie he made where everybody whistled?"

"*Bridge on the River Kwai.*"

"Raquel Welch and Kirk Douglas—that's an odd pair. Even without Kirk Douglas."

"Jesus, she's got enough chest to make three more Charlie's Angels."

"What's that she's got hanging around her neck?"

"A crucifix or an IUD."

"This show sucks."

"How old is Jane Powell[16]?"

"This things beginning to look like a tribute to the Motion Picture Relief Home."

"Whose idea was it to build stairs for these people? They should have built ramps."

"Why are they giving an Academy Award to a camera?"

"Because it can move without jiggling. Raquel will get one when she learns to do the same."

"Look, there's James Garner[17]. One goddam hour and the first real star to come on is selling a Polaroid."

"The director's having a tough time. Before, he had to find somebody in his seat enjoying himself. Now he has to try to find somebody *in* his seat."

"This thing's worse than the local Emmys."

"Well, there's good news and there's bad news. The good news is Jason Robards didn't show up; the bad news is Vanessa Redgrave did!"

"I've seen better fashion shows at Fedco."

"Why do they show the dresses from the films but not show clips of the nominated performers?"

"Why are they giving Charlton Heston the Humanitarian Award?"

"Because he promised not to make any more *Planet of the Apes* pictures."

"There's Sammy Davis[18]. After Vanessa and the Palestinians, they're giving equal time to the Jews."

"This must not be an important occasion; he's not wearing his jewelry."

"Oh…Have they found Charlie Chaplin's[19] body yet?"

"Jesus, Olivia de Havilland[20] must be 80, too."

"What's she done lately?

"Walked down those stairs."

"Whoever staged this Aretha Franklin[21] number must be trying to sell Hula-Hoops."

"Fred Astaire looks great for his age."

"What the hell is Cicely Tyson[22] wearing in her hair?"

"It looks like a lightning rod."

"Do you think *Annie Hall* deserves best picture?"

"It was all right."

"Woody Allen didn't show up, either."

"If these guys don't want to accept their Oscars, why don't they just withdraw from the nominations?"

"I'd like to see Presidential candidates do the same. Run for office, win, then refuse to show up at the inauguration."

"Jesus, listen to Paddy Chayefsky!"

"Go get 'em, Paddy. You're mad as hell and won't take it anymore."

"I admire that—a guy who makes a speech about why you shouldn't use the Academy Awards to make a speech."

"Christ, it looks like they booked Janet Gaynor[23] so they'd have somebody who looked older than Greer Garson[24]."

"Hell, she's a lot spunkier than most of them."

"What the hell is Diane Keaton wearing? It looks like she rented her outfit from Hobo Kelly."

"She really deserved the Oscar for *Goodbar*."

"Why is it that she can wear a dress in *The Godfather* and comes to the Awards looking like a reject from Goodwill?"

"In the movies she has to make believe; at the Awards she doesn't have to—she can be her own slobby self."

"Are they singing 'That's Entertainment'? Christ, that's almost as bad as listening to Jerry Lewis crying on cue at the end of this telethon."

After reading the Academy Awards feedback that John was privy to and shared with his readers, I was curious if he had any favorite actors or actresses. He did and provided me a list, albeit not a very long one, but a list nonetheless.

My all-time favorite actors:

1: Robert Donat in *Goodbye, Mr. Chips*

2: Cary Grant in anything.

3: Claude Rains.[25] The first actor to be paid a million dollars when he played Julius Caesar[26].

4: Richard Burton, until he married Liz Taylor and went from artist to celebrity.

5: Jack Nicholson in almost anything.

6: Bette Davis[27]. No one except Cary Grant comes close to the power of her performances…and personality!

7. James Mason

8. George Sanders[28]

Readers will notice that everyone on that list, except for Jack Nicholson, is no longer with us. And John has said that he doesn't go to the movies anymore so I asked him what he watches for entertainment, if anything.

"I scour PBS where I have found a number of shows I have loved: *Doc Martin, Victoria,* and *Atlantic Crossing*, all shows smart enough in every area to not only hold my attention but to recommend them to others."

I then wanted to know if there were any movie protagonists whose names that are known immediately without question? I actually had posed this question on social media and got literally hundreds of responses, many whose characters were first from a book. For John, though, he said, *Thelma and Louise*, Hannibal Lecter and Howard Beale.

It's been years since John last wrote movie reviews and went on to produce and host *Real People.*[29] He then made the documentaries *The JFK Assassination: The Jim Garrison Tapes* and *The American Media & The 2nd Assassination Of President John F. Kennedy.* Since I've known John now for several years and having worked on several projects with him, including two other books besides this one, it is apparent that keeping busy and creative has kept him young. What I've learned from him is to never give up. Anyone whose read his memoir will know what I mean. With that in mind, the following chapter is his "review" of when he traveled to shoot the first pilot for *Real People*, which was turned down by ABC. But John didn't give up and NBC bought it where it aired from 1979-1984. You can see clips of it on YouTube.

Notes

1 https://www.schickshadel.com/addictions/alcohol-addiction/
2 https://en.wikipedia.org/wiki/Liggett_Group
3 https://en.wikipedia.org/wiki/Bob_Abernethy
4 https://en.wikipedia.org/wiki/Howard_Beale_(Network)
5 https://en.wikipedia.org/wiki/Kelly_Lange
6 https://en.wikipedia.org/wiki/Paul_Moye
7 https://en.wikipedia.org/wiki/David_Horowitz
8 https://en.wikipedia.org/wiki/Tritia_Toyota
9 https://en.wikipedia.org/wiki/John_Simon_(critic)
10 https://en.wikipedia.org/wiki/Jim_Brown
11 https://en.wikipedia.org/wiki/Vanessa_Redgrave
12 https://en.wikipedia.org/wiki/Paul_Williams_(songwriter)
13 https://en.wikipedia.org/wiki/Debby_Boone
14 https://en.wikipedia.org/wiki/Barbara_Stanwyck
15 https://en.wikipedia.org/wiki/William_Holden
16 https://en.wikipedia.org/wiki/Jane_Powell
17 https://en.wikipedia.org/wiki/James_Garner
18 https://en.wikipedia.org/wiki/Sammy_Davis_Jr.
19 https://en.wikipedia.org/wiki/Charlie_Chaplin
20 https://en.wikipedia.org/wiki/Olivia_de_Havilland
21 https://en.wikipedia.org/wiki/Aretha_Franklin
22 https://en.wikipedia.org/wiki/Cicely_Tyson
23 https://en.wikipedia.org/wiki/Janet_Gaynor
24 https://en.wikipedia.org/wiki/Greer_Garson
25 https://en.wikipedia.org/wiki/Claude_Rains
26 https://en.wikipedia.org/wiki/Julius_Caesar
27 https://en.wikipedia.org/wiki/Bette_Davis
28 https://en.wikipedia.org/wiki/George_Sanders
29 https://en.wikipedia.org/wiki/Real_People

X. Film Critic At Large

WITH THE NATION'S INNKEEPER, ANY SURPRISE IS NO SURPRISE

By John Barbour

Our film critic's at large...and motel hopping

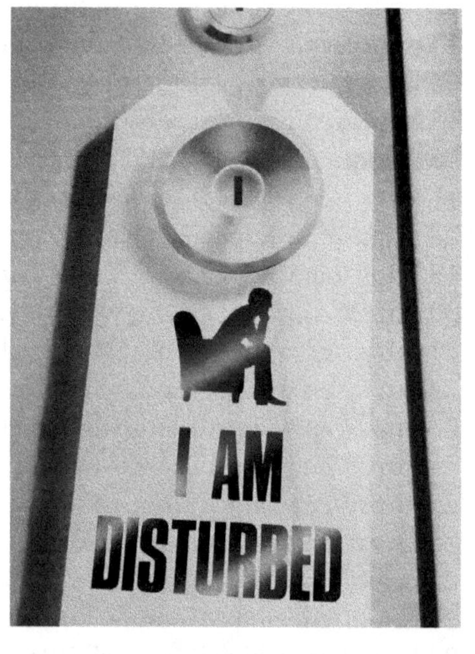

While traveling throughout America in September and October, gathering material for a TV show, I took a brief vacation from movie-going; so I'll give you a brief vacation from reading about movies, at least for a few paragraphs.

In all the years I've been reading *Los Angeles* magazine, I've always wondered how Frank Riley[1] is able to find so many places to enjoy. He is like the Charles Champlin of travel editors; no matter where he is, he will find something redeeming to say about it. Perhaps one of the reasons is that he has never stayed at a Holiday Inn. In traveling through 20 states in 20 days, our crew stayed at a dozen of them; the dirty dozen. Holiday Inns are like movies: You've got to go to 15 of them before you find one that's worth the money.

There were eight of us in the crew. No matter how carefully the clerks had registered us, callers were always informed that we had not checked in yet. We would have had an easier time getting our messages if they had been placed in a bottle and floated down the Mississippi. We would also have had an easier time getting our food that way. Nobody ever got a three-minute egg in less than an hour. Silverware took longer. We met only one efficient waitress: She had been on the job only a week, so she hadn't completed the training program. Dirty laundry could be sent out in the morning and returned that night, provided it didn't have to be cleaned.

The one we stayed at near Chicago's O'Hare Airport could have been used as one of the larger shacks in *Roots*. There was no elevator, which is probably why there was also no bellhop. I mean, who wants to carry somebody else's bags up the stairs? The cleaning people used a bug spray which must have been first tested in Vietnam; it could defoliate a forest and paralyze a herd of water buffalo. Unfortunately, they hadn't quite perfected its power to get rid of bugs—though it did manage to keep some of the guests away from their rooms while the locals were cleaning out their luggage. Our colleague, Emily Levine, had a couple of her silk blouses stolen while being kept at a distance by the bug spray; when she complained to the manager that two of her blouses had been taken, he consoled her by saying, "You should be glad they didn't take your life!"

The Holiday Inn in Chicago was the Waldorf, however, compared to the one in Daytona Beach. At the peak of the dinner hour we walked into its restaurant; there were three people there: the waitress, the cook and the cashier. We had an idea it might take a while to be served; next to the sign that read, optimistically, Please Wait to Be Seated was another that read, Checkout Time Is 11 a.m. The three employees stood around giggling for a while, then explained their behavior by saying they had never seen anyone before who sounded like us. When we asked what we sounded like, they said, "*Customahs*!"

Twenty minutes after ordering it, I got my glass of Burgundy. I didn't know Bitter Lemon had bought a winery! I told the woman it was sour.

Fifteen minutes later she brought it back and said, "The bahtendah says no it ayn't." I told her firmly to take it back and bring me another glass. Fifteen minutes later she returned. The wine was still bitter; I informed her that it tasted the same, and she replied, "Y'all jes said yah wanted another *glass*."

Not wanting to hassle with anyone who had obviously graduated from the Idi Amin school of bartending, we ordered dinner. The menu advertised mushrooms, but only served mushroom—one single mushroom atop some peas. You were able to distinguish the gray mushroom from the gray peas because it had a stem on it. I ordered the seafood plate. It *was* seafood in a way: It was bait. Two of the others in the crew ordered aged steak. We guessed it was aged when we found gray hairs on it. Unable to tolerate the ineptness any longer, we asked to speak to the manager. We were informed there was no food manager. The last one had quit. Perhaps this Holiday Inn had offered him room and board, and all he wanted was the room.

We were told, though, that there was a little card in our rooms that encouraged customers to make comments about the food and service. This card had a happy face on it, a sad face and a blank oval on which we were supposed to draw an expression that corresponded to our feelings about our stay there. But there were no pens. Fortunately, we had brought our own, and we filled the blank oval with bubbles, garbage and gas and drew lines attaching it to the sad face. Underneath, where it requested remarks, we wrote that in case there was any doubt about how sick our stay at this Holiday Inn was, we were enclosing the x-rays of our stomachs.

We did come across one really excellent Holiday Inn in the Southeast. This one also inadvertently provided us with one of our merrier moments.

One of the people we were going to tape on the trip was an old man who claims he's the unluckiest man alive. At the age of three he was shot in the face by his brother. At six his father split his skull with an ax. His family never had him wear clothes; he wore targets. He had been run over, stomped on and crushed. His first wife, an alcoholic, shot him in the chest and arm. His second wife and her lover tried to murder him for his mobile home.

The day before we were to talk to Mr. Lucky in his home town, we got held up by the weather 200 miles away, after videotaping a religious-political backwoods commune populated by people who've renounced industrial America in order to live like cavemen. Their only modern convenience is a rifle. Since we would be unable to fly the equipment up to do the interview with Mr. Lucky, we called him and offered to fly him to town, where we would do the interview at our Holiday Inn near the airport. He accepted. That night, though, we discovered we could not even get the equipment back from the commune and into town. In order to do the interview with Mr. Lucky, we would have to drive him *there*.

The next morning when we met him at the airport, we did not have the heart to tell him exactly where we had to take him. He was told there had been a slight change in plans and that we would now have to do the interview at a quaint tourist attraction down the road a piece. (Down the road a piece was 80 miles.) He fell asleep, and woke up just as we turned off the highway onto the narrow, bumpy dirt road that led into the forest. His eyes got the size of headlights as we approached the compound. He couldn't believe what he was seeing: scores of people walking around dressed like Tarzan and Jane and Adam and Eve. They looked like they lived in huts or holes, and one of them was carrying a rifle. After a moment Lucky gasped, "What the hell kind of Holiday Inn is this?"

When we explained how he had happened to end up there, he said, "Boy, fer a minute, when I saw that guy with the rifle, I thought y'all was from *This is Yer Life* and y'all was brangin' me tuh a family reunion!"

Afterward, at a bar, we all collapsed with laughter when we realized just how unlucky this old man was. The one really good Holiday Inn we had found, and he never had a chance to see it!

Before our caravan reached New York we decided that, in order to save our sanity and Emily's clothes, we should take a vacation from Holiday Inns and stay someplace else. The place we chose was a fairly well-known hotel overlooking Central Park.

Fred Allen used to joke about a New York hotel room he had stayed in that was so small the mice were hunchbacked; I never understood that joke until I saw our room. Of course, we didn't find any hunchbacked mice; there was no room for mice. All we found was a cockroach that slouched a lot—and was responsible, at least, for us getting a free room. The elevator was larger than our living quarters. One of the guys who ordered room service ended up having to eat in the hall. The closet had space enough for one suit—provided you didn't fold the pants. And if you left the closet door open, you couldn't open the door to the room.

The bed was a cot. It was shoved up against the left wall to make room for the Tonka Toy dresser shoved up against the right wall. If the drawers were open you couldn't walk in between. The window, which was a little wider than a rearview mirror, was at the foot of the bed. It was the only thing you left open—in case you were asleep and you wanted to stretch your legs without cutting your ankles on broken glass. The TV set was also at the foot of the bed—on rollers.

In order to get to the bathroom, you had to move the TV set between the cot and the dresser. If one of the dresser drawers was left open, you didn't go.

The bathroom itself was designed for a male Munchkin who could do everything standing because God forbid you should try to sit down! The walls were so thin that at any moment I expected some guy to stick his head through the medicine cabinet shouting, "Hi, guy. How's your

Right Guard?" In order to get into these rooms we needed a reservation. In order to get out of them we needed an engineering degree.

It was on our second day in New York that I caught *The Boys from Brazil*, starring Laurence Olivier and Gregory Peck.[2] I should have stayed in my room. The film was made by 20th Century-Fox but looked like it was subcontracted to AIP. What starts out as a story about Nazis ends up as sloppy sci-fi.

A young American Jew living in Paraguay discovers that a group of Nazi war criminals is about to assassinate 94 non-Jewish civil servants around the world, all of them 65 years old. He finds out this information by bugging one of the Nazi's estates after befriending one of the guards, a 10-year-old native. And if you believe that a wealthy Nazi fugitive would have a 10-year-old native opening and closing the gate to his armored estate, you'd believe W.E. B. was a hit.

The bug is discovered, and the young American is killed while telephoning Olivier, an aging Nazi hunter living in Europe. Even though the Nazis know Olivier received the call, and even though they killed 6 million Jews in the past and are about to do in 94 Gentiles now, they don't bother trying to eliminate Olivier because James Mason as the head of the security thinks some people might get the idea that Nazis are up to no good.

As the civil servants begin meeting mysterious deaths, Olivier begins to visit the widows. He soon discovers that each set of parents had adopted a clone of Adolf Hitler. Even though these clones, who are now 14 years old, come from differing backgrounds, director Franklin Schaffner[3] has invested them all with one distinctive character trait: They are all snotty. If Schaffner is subtle, Jimmy Carter[4] has no teeth.

James Mason discovers Olivier is really onto the plot; but instead of going after him, he goes after Gregory Peck—the doctor who developed the clones. The plot is called off, but Peck hightails it to the States to do in one of the civil servants on his own. We know this because he wrote it down on his office wall. Germans always did have a thing about keeping records.

Olivier's performance is the only thing in *The Boys from Brazil* that is not entirely laughable, but even he is soon done in by Schaffner's sloppiness and the script's silliness. Following a fight scene in which Peck bites off Olivier's ear, we see Olivier in the hospital the next moment with it intact. It was a wasted act in any case. The way Peck chews on the dialogue, he could have just talked it off.

Notes
1 https://en.wikipedia.org/wiki/Frank_Riley_(author)
2 https://en.wikipedia.org/wiki/Gregory_Peck
3 https://en.wikipedia.org/wiki/Franklin_J._Schaffner
4 https://en.wikipedia.org/wiki/Jimmy_Carter

REAL
PEOPLE

Having worked with John on his memoir, I know how much he wanted *Real People* to succeed and I cannot help but think that movie viewers who relied on John for his critiques lost something in the process. Even now, all these years later, I wish John would once again treat us to his wonderful comments regarding movie releases. He wouldn't even need to leave his home now that there are numerous streaming possibilities. However, take heart, because John is now in the process of working on a podcast called *Talking Movies*. I, for one, am eager to listen in since I know it will be entertaining and informative.

Also, while I was reading the bios of the many people who were referenced in this book, many who have died years ago or just recently, I found myself feeling saddened to think that they won't be making any more movies, whether in front of or behind the camera. They had their moment and yet, for good or bad, they have left us with their works on celluloid, most that we can still watch to this day.

That said, I am grateful John brought those movies to my attention. There are so many more reviews that John sent me but it wasn't possible to include them all. Perhaps, though, they may show up in some form or another in the future. But for now, I hope you enjoyed reading many of the *Greatest Reviews I Ever Read*!

Carol Hoenig

JOHN BARBOUR is recognized as 'The Godfather of Reality TV' as the creator-producer, co-host, and writer of the trendsetting hit *Real People*. He won the first of his 5 Emmys as the original Host of 'AM LA' in 1970 where he interviewed controversial anti-war guests like Mohammed Ali, Cesar Chavez and Jane Fonda. He was the first in America to do film reviews on the news, winning 3 more consecutive Emmys as KNBC's Critic-At-Large and ten years as *Los Angeles Magazine's* most widely read and quoted controversial critic. Prior to that he was a successful topical stand-up comedian, appearing on *The Dean Martin Show, The Tonight Show*, and others. He is the author of Your Mother's Not a Virgin: The Bumpy Life and Times of the Canadian Dropout Who Changed the Face of American TV. You may find out more about John at https://johnbarboursworld.com.

CAROL HOENIG is President of Carol Hoenig, Publishing Consultant, Inc. and the author of the Without Grace, Of Little Faith, and The Author's Guide To Planning Book Events. Her essays, articles, book reviews and short stories appear in a wide number of publications. You may find out more about her at carolhoenig.com.

CPSIA information can be obtained
at www.ICGtesting.com
Printed in the USA
LVHW081931031021
699414LV00004B/16

9 780578 990231